1. Who Do You Say That I Am?

WHO DO YOU SAY THAT I AM?

AN ADULT INQUIRY INTO THE
FIRST THREE GOSPELS

WHO DO YOU SAY THAT I AM?

Edward J. Ciuba

SECOND REVISED EDITION

ALBA · HOUSE   NEW · YORK

SOCIETY OF ST. PAUL, 2187 VICTORY BLVD., STATEN ISLAND, NY 10314

Scripture quotations from the Gospels are taken from *The Alba House Gospels: So You May Believe,* translated by Mark A. Wauck (New York: Alba House, 1992).

Library of Congress Cataloging-in-Publication Data

   Ciuba, Edward J., 1935-
     Who do you say that I am? : an adult inquiry into the first three
   Gospels / Edward J. Ciuba. — 2nd rev. ed.
       p.   cm.
     Includes bibliographical references.
     ISBN 0-8189-0638-3
     1. Bible. N.T. Gospels — Criticism, interpretation, etc.
   2. Bible. N.T. Matthew — Criticism, interpretation, etc. 3. Bible.
   N.T. Mark — Criticism, interpretation, etc. 4. Bible. N.T. Luke —
   Criticism, interpretation, etc.   I. Title.
   BS2555.2.C54   1993
   282'.06 — dc20   92-37734
                                          CIP

Produced and designed in the United States of America by the
Fathers and Brothers of the Society of St. Paul,
2187 Victory Boulevard, Staten Island, New York 10314,
as part of their communications apostolate.

ISBN: 0-8189-0638-3

Printing Information:

Current Printing - first digit	1	2	3	4	5	6	7	8	9	10

Year of Current Printing - first year shown

1993	1994	1995	1996	1997	1998

TABLE OF CONTENTS

BIBLICAL ABBREVIATIONS

Old Testament

Genesis	Gn	Nehemiah	Ne	Baruch	Ba
Exodus	Ex	Tobit	Tb	Ezekiel	Ezk
Leviticus	Lv	Judith	Jdt	Daniel	Dn
Numbers	Nb	Esther	Est	Hosea	Ho
Deuteronomy	Dt	1 Maccabees	1 M	Joel	Jl
Joshua	Jos	2 Maccabees	2 M	Amos	Am
Judges	Jg	Job	Jb	Obadiah	Ob
Ruth	Rt	Psalms	Ps	Jonah	Jon
1 Samuel	1 S	Proverbs	Pr	Micah	Mi
2 Samuel	2 S	Ecclesiastes	Ec	Nahum	Na
1 Kings	1 K	Song of Songs	Sg	Habakkuk	Hab
2 Kings	2 K	Wisdom	Ws	Zephaniah	Zp
1 Chronicles	1 Ch	Sirach	Si	Haggai	Hg
2 Chronicles	2 Ch	Isaiah	Is	Malachi	Ml
Ezra	Ezr	Jeremiah	Jr	Zechariah	Zc
		Lamentations	Lm		

New Testament

Matthew	Mt	Ephesians	Ep	Hebrews	Heb
Mark	Mk	Philippians	Ph	James	Jm
Luke	Lk	Colossians	Col	1 Peter	1 P
John	Jn	1 Thessalonians	1 Th	2 Peter	2 P
Acts	Ac	2 Thessalonians	2 Th	1 John	1 Jn
Romans	Rm	1 Timothy	1 Tm	2 John	2 Jn
1 Corinthians	1 Cor	2 Timothy	2 Tm	3 John	3 Jn
2 Corinthians	2 Cor	Titus	Tt	Jude	Jude
Galatians	Gal	Philemon	Phm	Revelation	Rv

FOREWORD

Our times give evidence of a deep hunger for Jesus. Who is he? Does he have any meaning for our lives? Whatever the reasons — whether the constant change and hectic pace so endemic to our society, the many pressures created by the complexity of modern living, or simply a general disenchantment with institutions and churches — Christians are yearning for a deeper, more personal experience of God. They are unhappy with the impersonality and the assembly-line approach projected by many of our large churches. They are looking for a more personal message, one of honesty, simplicity and integrity.

Reacting against dull, impersonal forms of piety, younger Christians, especially, are showing an avid, if eclectic, interest in religion, in ways as diverse as the New Age movement and fundamentalism to the practice of Yoga, Zen and Oriental methods of meditation. They are looking for new forms to restore some semblance of inner peace to their lives, and to offset the chaos and fragmentation that is so much a part of the culture of our Western society. Their quest of the "meaningful" is spoken of so frequently that the phrase has become a well-worn cliché. The fact of the matter is: many people are looking to fill a void in their lives. But how?

For Christians, regardless of age, this quest for meaning and for a personal orientation to Jesus Christ has brought them to the refreshing source of the biblical Word. More and more they are filling that void by drawing sustenance from the Scriptures, the words of life. Clear testimony to this renewed interest in the

Scriptures is given by the sudden and prolific emergence of so many different groups focusing on Bible reading, Scripture discussion and prayerful reflection on God's Word. In trying to avoid the shallowness and artificiality of much that passes as important in our society, more and more people are growing in the appreciation of a Word that gives direction and meaning to their life.

During these past few decades, nowhere has this interest and enthusiasm for God's Word been so strikingly evident, as in the Roman Catholic tradition. Until recently, Scripture reading and Bible study were generally regarded as Protestant practices, at least on the popular level. Catholics were not known for their interest in or knowledge of the Bible. One would honestly have to say that one of the more tragic consequences of the Protestant Reformation was a neglect of the Bible among the Catholic faithful. While it was never completely forgotten, the Bible was a closed book for most Catholics. They placed greater reliance on Church teachings, structure and ecclesiastical discipline. Among twentieth-century Catholics, the Bible has attained a popularity unrivalled in centuries past.

Two important factors have contributed to this rebirth of the Scriptures. The first was Pius XII's encyclical *Divino Afflante Spiritu* of 1943, which inaugurated the greatest renewal in the study of the Bible that the Roman Catholic Church has ever seen. The encouraging and positive tone of the encyclical gave Catholic scholars a green light for utilizing the modern tools of literary criticism and applying them properly for a better, more nuanced understanding of the Bible. Since that time, great strides have been made. Scripture scholars accepted with enthusiasm the invitation extended by Pope Pius XII, and their untiring efforts since then have had far reaching implications. Today, Catholic, Protestant and Jewish scholars, working hand in hand on a variety of different projects, are producing ever more accurate translations of the Bible based on original texts; they share one another's research and cooperate with one another toward a more faithful interpretation of the Bible and a wider dissemination of its riches.

The second factor grew out of the goals and purposes of the Second Vatican Council. The Council gave the Church a golden opportunity to take a good look at itself as in a mirror and to ask itself some pointed questions. Was the image seen a faithful reflection of what Jesus intended for his Church, or was that image smudged and stained with the passage of time? Was the mission of the Church faithful to the wishes of its founder? Were the teaching and practice of the Church patterned faithfully on the norms set down by Jesus Christ or had they become tarnished by certain human accretions inconsistent with the intent of their founder? Where else could one search for answers to these provoking questions if not in God's revelatory Word and in the ongoing tradition which interprets it? Hence the vital importance of the Scriptures.

The influence of the Scriptures, as well as a distinct biblical tone, is apparent in virtually all of the conciliar formulations. To cite a few examples: *The Dogmatic Constitution on Divine Revelation* is premised upon the core value of the Scriptures for teaching and preaching. For the first time in centuries, the Church is openly encouraging the use of the Scriptures for the life and practice of its members. In the all-important *Dogmatic Constitution on the Church* the identity and structure of the Church are set forth, not through the formulation of new definitions, but through the use of certain time-honored biblical images such as the People of God, the Body of Christ, the sheepfold, the vineyard of God, the temple of the Holy Spirit, the pilgrim community. Since the Church is a mystery, it can, of course, never be exhaustively defined, but its nature is best communicated by studying these metaphors which reveal its essential characteristics.

Liturgical renewal has not only increased the number of Scripture readings at Sunday Mass and arranged them in cycles for wider exposure, but the signs and symbols of the sacred rites themselves have been given added clarity and sharpness by a recognition of their profound and authentic biblical roots. The basis for ecumenical dialogue with our non-Catholic brothers and sisters is, and must always be, the biblical Word, a rich common heritage from which grows mutual respect and understanding. Our much neglected relationship with the Jews can only be enhanced by our recognition that the God of Abraham, Isaac and Jacob is also the God of Jesus Christ. The God of the Old Testament is the same God whom we as Christians address daily as "Our Father." The responsibilities that we have to the poor, the deprived and the underprivileged, so ably formulated in the *Pastoral Constitution on the Church in the Modern World*, are traceable to the strong communal dimension of biblical revelation.

As the Council gave the Church an opportunity to look at itself in light of the biblical Word, so also the members of the Church have had to do the same. Priests, religious and lay people are asking basic questions about their identity as Christians, about their mission, ministry and lifestyle, about the quality of response asked of them because of their faith and commitment to Jesus. All are called to holiness; all are called to serve; all are called to give faithful witness to the Lord, although the approaches of each may vary. It is becoming more and more evident that Christians are looking to the Scriptures for an answer to their questions and they are hoping to find in them the basis for a more personal experience of God in the person and Word of his Son, Jesus Christ.

GENERAL AIMS AND PURPOSES

The purpose of this book is closely connected with what has just been said: to reveal the rich experience of Jesus Christ as recounted in the first three Gospels.

Two principles underlie the approach taken:

1. This book is meant for those who are approaching the Gospels for the first time.
2. It incorporates sound biblical scholarship adapted to beginners.

My experience has been that readers approaching the Scriptures for the first time, even with the best of intentions, do not really know where to begin or how to go about it. The Bible is so vast and reflects the faith of so many centuries that, without some initial guidance, a person can easily become confused and/or frustrated.

Paradoxically, even the great advances in biblical scholarship intended ultimately to clarify the Scriptures, sometimes serve the opposite purpose and become a hindrance for beginners. Because they have not had the time or the leisure for advanced biblical studies, beginners are sometimes thwarted and frightened away by the technical jargon and terminology that frequently accompanies a critical approach to the Scriptures. Study of the Bible sometimes becomes a stuffy and dull exercise when a lot of time and energy is spent talking *about* the Bible, without ever getting to the actual experience communicated therein. People today are not so much interested in a bookish or academic approach to the Scriptures as they are in sharing its rich personal message and experience. Sometimes the impression is given that one must be a proficient biblical scholar to enjoy the vitality and meaning of God's Word. Not so!

In saying this, however, we have no intention of demeaning the painful work of scholars, or of minimizing the vital importance of critical scholarship. After all, one cannot read through a book which is more than 1900 years old in the same way one would read through a modern magazine. For this reason some spadework into the background of the biblical writings is a necessity. Furthermore, an unwillingness to pursue critical methods of Bible study may lead to a deadening fundamentalism or a woodenly literal interpretation of the text, which does justice neither to God nor to the communicators of God's Word.

Critical scholarship does not have to be dull and academic. The time is ripe, as perhaps never before, for utilizing the vast amount of contemporary scholarship in a truly pastoral manner so that the immense riches of the Bible will have practical import for the ordinary reader. If used effectively, modern biblical scholarship can bring out the vitality and personal dimensions of God's Word. It can sharpen and hone that "two-edged sword" spoken of by the author of the letter to the Hebrews which "penetrates and divides soul and spirit, joints and marrow, and judges the reflections and thoughts of the heart" (Heb 4:12).

My purpose here is to utilize the best critical tools, methods and conclusions of contemporary scholarship and then to apply them to the Gospels in such a way that the ordinary layperson will better appreciate the power, vitality and freshness of God's Word. This book is aimed at helping the reader better to answer that question directed to every disciple of Jesus: "And you, who do you say that I am?"

The Particular Aims and Purposes of This Book

1. As mentioned before, this book is addressed to adult and inquiring readers who are approaching the New Testament Scriptures for the first time. All of us have some acquaintance with the Scriptures, either from personal reading or from hearing them proclaimed in the context of the liturgy. But to go beyond the literal meaning of the words — as important as they are — and to ascertain the intention of the biblical author for using the words he did, some further assistance may be necessary.

An adult approach to the Scriptures demands that today's reader know something about the context in which the Scriptures were written: the language, thought patterns, historical and cultural background, and the organic process of growth and development from an oral stage to final articulation in written form. The Gospels, for example, were written in Palestine in the first century A.D., more than 1900 years ago. As is evident, some background work is necessary before the intention of the biblical authors when writing about Jesus can accurately be determined.

2. The eight chapters in this book are limited to the significant dimensions of the first three Gospels. The Gospels according to Matthew, Mark and Luke are called the "Synoptic Gospels" ("synoptic" comes from a Greek word meaning "to view together"), because they can be set side-by-side and read together. The Gospel according to John is very different in outline, content and style.

A fundamental premise of the book is that the best way for beginners to approach the New Testament Scriptures — and the entire Bible for that matter — is to begin with the Synoptic

Gospels. It is there that we have the heart and core of the revelation of God in the person and message of Jesus Christ. The rest of the Scriptures are like the petals of a flower, unfurling out of a central core and giving meaning to the other books of the Bible. Even the Old Testament will be appreciated and understood better as the "first covenant" once the reader understands the way in which the Gospel authors interpreted its themes of fulfillment in light of the person of Jesus.

Occasionally, reference is made to the Gospel according to John, especially in the last chapter on the resurrection. However, when reference is made to the "Gospels," the first three Gospels are to be understood unless otherwise stated.

3. This book tries to convey the experience of the Gospels in a popularized fashion and in ordinary, down-to-earth language. So many explanations of the Gospels become obfuscated with scientific jargon and terminology that the reader can be frightened away and despair of ever arriving at an adequate comprehension of the Bible. While care has been taken to incorporate the vast amount of critical information available, I have tried to translate this important information and research into the ordinary language of the lay person.

This work, intended for general use, abridges, simplifies and reduces to a popular level, matters which are sometimes complex and nuanced. Certain areas may be questioned, but options are permissible. When choosing one of these options, I am not unaware of other possibilities. But the option chosen is always well founded. One has to begin somewhere. To include all possible opinions and options can lead to digressions beyond the limited scope of a work like this. For this reason, a *Select Bibliography* is offered at the end of the book for the reader who wants to pursue a given point in greater detail.

4. While this book may be used effectively by individuals, it has been prepared with group discussion in mind. The reasoning behind this is twofold:

First, though group discussions on the Bible are quite common today, very often there is no *practical* text available to be used as a guideline. This book will meet that need.

Second, the interaction of a group — discussing, sharing, affirming and even disagreeing — almost always results in a number of insights that might easily be overlooked by any one individual.

Another reason for the group approach is based on the premise that the Gospels were the response of the first-century followers of Jesus to the words and deeds of their leader. The Gospels, as we shall see, grew out of the Church and were intended for use by the Church. That vision will be appreciated in greater depth by the communal sharing and interaction of men and women who are also members of the Church. Each chapter concludes with questions for discussion and suggested readings.

5. Last, and most important, this book tries to capture the experience of those first disciples, apostles and evangelists who were confronted with the reality of Jesus Christ. The key word is *experience*. We are trying to translate the *experience* of those first disciples of Jesus into our own living experience.

Therefore, this is not a commentary on the Scriptures, or a verse-by-verse explanation of the biblical text. Neither is this presentation concerned with the central themes of the Gospels, although at times they will enter into our discussions. Nor is it within the scope of this book to try to write a biography or a spiritual history of Jesus — an almost impossible task as we shall see — although there will be material enough for spiritual reflection.

This work is based on an understanding of the Gospels as *faith testimonies*, written accounts of the faith and experience of the early Christian community. Something about Jesus Christ and his message jolted his followers, evoked in them a response, engendered a way of thinking and acting, and gave rise to a strong personal experience which they then communicated in words. Like us, they too were trying to respond to the question: "Who do you say that I am?" Hopefully, our sharing in that experience of the first disciples will give meaning and purpose to our own efforts to make sense out of our lives.

HOW TO USE THIS BOOK

For an effective use of this book, the reader is encouraged to follow these steps:

1. Before each chapter, read the biblical texts assigned.

2. Read through the contents of the assigned chapter and try to make applications to the biblical text.

3. Jot down any questions which require elaboration or clarification.

4. Read through the *Questions for Discussion* at the end of each chapter and try to determine how you would answer them.

5. Assign a leader who will direct the discussion for each chapter. The ideal discussion leader is one who has already had some acquaintance with the Gospels.

6. The discussion leader may present all the questions one by one, if time permits. Otherwise, those questions may be discussed which have particular interest or significance for the group.

7. Those points which still remain unclear may be pursued by referring to the *Select Bibliography* at the end of the book.

8. A summary should be made of the significant points discussed. (If the chapter content strikes the interest of the group more than usual, it should be treated again at another session.)

9. More important than following these steps rigidly is to ask yourself what the Scriptures are saying to you personally. How would you respond to the question, "Who do you say that I am?"

RECOMMENDED SCRIPTURE READINGS

Once acquainted with the biblical text, the reader will derive great enjoyment and profit from these studies. The first three chapters presuppose a prior reading of the Gospels according to Matthew, Mark and Luke. The reader is also urged to reread a number of relevant Gospel passages (cited below) highlighting the content of each chapter.

	MARK	MATTHEW	LUKE
Chapter I	1-16		
Chapter II		1 - 28	
Chapter III			1 - 24
Chapter IV	1:1-45;	3 - 4; 11:2-15;	3 - 4
Chapter V	4;	13; 20:1-16;	11:33-36; 12 - 20
Chapter VI	1:23, 2:12; 3:1-30; 5; 6; 8:1-30;	8 - 9; 14:13-36; 15:21-39;	11:14-26
Chapter VII	12:28-34;	5; 7; 19:16-30; 22:34-40;	6:17-49; 10:25-37
Chapter VIII	16:1-20; John 20 - 21 1 Corinthians 15	28:1-20;	24;

WHO DO YOU SAY THAT I AM?

THE BIRTH OF THE GOSPEL

Mark 1 - 16

*A*nyone who wants to know more about the life and times of prominent historical figures — let us say, men like Napoleon Bonaparte, Mahatma Gandhi, or one of our distinguished American presidents like Abraham Lincoln — has access to a vast amount of resource material: histories, biographies, memoirs, documentaries, newspaper clippings and sometimes even photographs. There is no end to the quality and amount of information available about such men. The problem, if any, is one of abundance. A reader would have to be very selective and discriminate so as to choose wisely from among the various resources, because not all of them would be suitable.

But what sources are available to us for researching the life of Jesus of Nazareth? Unfortunately, the ample documentary material readily obtainable for a Napoleon, Gandhi or Lincoln is not as abundant or available for Jesus. It is not that resources are lacking but that they are qualitatively different. Our main sources are the New Testament Scriptures: documents of faith, written testimonies to the Lordship of Jesus, accounts recorded "so you may believe that Jesus is the Messiah, the Son of God, and so that by believing you may have life in his name" (Jn 20:31). Both in form and content the New Testament Scriptures are an inspiring body of religious literature about a truly unique historical person, but they are hardly adequate materials for a detailed biography of Jesus.

1

What about extra-biblical sources? Do they offer any evidence for the life and times of Jesus? Pagan histories of the first century are not much help either in this regard; they tell us little of Jesus, apart from the fact that he lived and died. Other related works, like the Jewish historical literature of that period, yield very little factual information, other than mentioning the followers of Jesus and his death at Passover. They tell us nothing about the many interesting biographical details that would have provided excellent material for a life of Jesus: his infancy and adolescent years, his preaching and healings, the account of his death and resurrection, his establishment of a community of disciples to continue his work.

Perhaps the writers of the first century were prejudiced against him — an assumption with some foundation. Maybe religious preachers and reformers in remote, forlorn Palestine were not newsworthy. Whatever the reason, the point is: there is scant information about Jesus of Nazareth in the extra-biblical literature of the first century A.D.

We are thus left with the New Testament itself as the chief source from which to learn more about Jesus. While extra-biblical data may be meager, there is no reason for skepticism or uneasiness. There were other religious reformers and messianic pretenders in Palestine during the first century A.D. Only the passage of time would bear out the distinguishable and significant features of Jesus of Nazareth and the import of his message for subsequent history. For the Jews, he was another religious upstart; for the Romans, another Jewish revolutionary. After all, does a common criminal, whose ultimate fate was crucifixion, provide exciting copy for Jewish or Roman history?

More important for our purposes, however, is an investigation of the New Testament documents themselves as sources for our understanding of the person and nature of Jesus. As subsequent investigation will reveal, the New Testament was never intended to be a strict biography or critical history. However, it does capture the meaning and significance of a unique historical person whose message and ideals are of vital concern to millions of people today.

WHERE DOES ONE BEGIN?

If, then, the New Testament itself is the principal source from which to learn more about Jesus, where does one begin? The question is a valid one. Considering the number and variety of books in the New Testament (twenty-seven in all), different options are available. For practical purposes, however, they can be reduced to two: the letters of St. Paul and the Gospel accounts of the life and ministry of Jesus.

Our inquiry into the life of Jesus will begin with the latter. While Paul's letters may have been the earliest New Testament documents set down in writing (his first letter to the Thessalonians dates from around 51 A.D., only twenty years after the death and resurrection of the Lord), they are not concerned with the life and ministry of Jesus. Paul writes about the manner of living demanded of Jesus' followers. He exhorts, encourages, pleads, redresses or admonishes, as called for by the particular situations of the early Christian communities.

Writing to the Thessalonians, for example, Paul addresses himself to the confused situation of those who were expecting the imminent return of the Lord, ushering in the final times. Apparently this problem continued to preoccupy the Thessalonians when Paul wrote again several months later. He chided them for their apathy and listlessness and told them, in effect, not to sit around doing nothing while waiting for the Lord to return on the clouds of heaven, but to get back to their normal day-to-day routines.

In his first letter to the Corinthians (written around 56 A.D.), Paul responds to certain problems which had cropped up there as well: open factionalism among the Church members, certain scandalous immoral practices, legal conflicts, quarrels over women's rights at liturgical gatherings, abuse in the use of charisms, and denial by some of bodily resurrection.

The same holds true for the remaining epistles of Paul: the prime concern of the letters is always the Christian lifestyle. Paul sees the need to convince newly-converted Christians of the significance of the Risen Lord in their lives. But in doing so, he gives us no clear picture or account of the life and ministry of Jesus.

We return then to the Gospels. In form and content they offer more details about Jesus' mission than do any of the Pauline epistles. Because they are recorded later, however, they are farther removed from the lifetime of Jesus. Paul, for example, wrote his letters between 51-61 A.D. while the *earliest* of the written Gospels, that of Mark, was not set down in writing until 65-68 A.D.; those of Matthew and Luke were finally recorded some fifteen to twenty years later. Obviously, then, the earliest of the Gospels was not recorded until some thirty or thirty-five years after the actual events of Jesus' life. In the case of Matthew and Luke, fifty years or more elapsed before their Gospels were completed. Today, any serious inquiry into the Gospels must take into account the growth and development of the words and deeds of Jesus from the time they actually occurred, around 30-33 A.D., to the time of their final recording by the evangelists many years later.

The Human Element of the Gospels

To appreciate the difference between the historical event and the subsequent interpretation of that event is to respect the human element of the Scriptures. We so often emphasize the Scriptures as God's Word that we may not always appreciate the human element involved in the formulation of that Word. As the next two chapters will reveal in detail, there was a long and vital period of transmission — both oral and written — when the Jesus traditions were preached, adapted, reformulated and transformed by preachers and missionaries before they were finally set down in written form by the evangelists.

In substance, this is the central preoccupation of what is generally referred to as the "historical-critical" approach to the Gospels. The ominous-sounding tone of this expression means simply that any early document, to be interpreted and understood correctly, must be examined in the light of the historical, literary and cultural context in which it was written. Would we ever understand the mind of Napoleon, or the significance of Gandhi, or recognize the strength of Lincoln's character without examining the historical background of the times in which these men lived, or without evaluating the records which tell us about them?

The same holds true for Jesus in the Gospels. His words and deeds did not fall miraculously from heaven; they were not transmitted by means of a celestial dictaphone. His words must, therefore, be interpreted in light of the language, verbal patterns and formulations of first century Palestine (*literary criticism*). The deeds he performed must be examined in the light of the historical context in which he lived: the religious outlook of his contemporaries, the political circumstances of the times, the cultural and social background, etc. (*historical criticism*). Since God became truly incarnate in the person of his Son, Jesus Christ, the human dimension must be respected. Furthermore, the significance of this God-man was interpreted through the minds, hearts, emotions, feelings and words of human beings — people like ourselves.

There should be no cause for concern in subjecting documents like the Gospels to "historical criticism." After all, such "criticism" (coming from the Greek word *krinein*, meaning to judge or evaluate), simply recognizes that God's Word comes to us through the words of humans like ourselves. The Scriptures were not oracular utterances from heaven; they were not written in a vacuum. They are the words of people specially chosen for this task, living in definite historical and cultural circumstances, and writing in a language spoken by Palestinians of the first century. The end result is a body of writing, subject to the evaluation and investigation proper to any body of literature written by human authors, even if they are inspired.

To be faithful, then, to the intention of the inspired writers (and so understand what God has revealed through them), we must allow them to speak out of their own historical, living context, instead of reading into the text our own twentieth-century background. Otherwise, we run the risk of falling into "fundamentalism," a grossly simplistic and literal interpretation of the text which does justice neither to God nor to the Gospel writers responsible for God's Word.

In conclusion, a "critical" approach to the Gospels allows the sacred authors to speak for themselves, instead of imposing on them our own twentieth-century views and interpretations. Though *sacred* authors, they are also people of their times, using the common language of their times, and preaching Jesus as Lord and Messiah in a manner most suited to the specific needs and circumstances of their times. When the historical and literary context of these writings is not respected, then the voice of the biblical authors grows weak and inaudible. So, too, does God's Word speaking through them.

The critical approach helps today's reader better appreciate the importance of that relatively long period of time when the words and deeds of Jesus were being modified, adapted and transformed, before being permanently fixed in the evangelists' texts. The picture of Jesus is prismed through the living faith and experience of the early Christian community. In the following pages, we hope to capture that experience of Jesus, as it confronted and challenged his contemporaries, and to make it our own. This is how believers today can "come to know Jesus Christ." Before reaching that step, however, it will be necessary to outline in detail some of the earlier oral stages of Gospel formation.

PRIORITY OF THE ORAL GOSPEL

Initially the Gospel was *preached*. As mentioned previously, more than thirty years ensued after the death and resurrection of Jesus before the Gospels were written down. The word *Gospel* really means *Good News!* It is the good news of God's intervention in time and history in the person of his Son, Jesus Christ. Israel's long period of waiting was over; many years of intense anticipation had come to a happy end. *Good News* indeed! A new age had dawned; the long-awaited Messiah had come; the "reign of sin was ended and a broken world was once again made whole." The gates of paradise were opened to God's faithful people who were promised eternal life in the hereafter.

Such was the basic message of the first preachers and missionaries soon after the death and resurrection of Jesus. They began to tell how God's mercy and love for all had been revealed in the person of Jesus. A new relationship with God was now possible by placing one's faith in Jesus and his message, through a radical change of mind and heart and, ultimately by baptism into the community of believers.

But this new, vital and hopeful message was not read in newspapers or taught in classrooms. It was not relegated to scholars. It was preached; it spread about quickly by word-of-mouth. Like people who have suddenly and unexpectedly come upon good fortune and have to tell everyone about it, so too the first disciples, empowered by the Holy Spirit, went out and proclaimed openly and enthusiastically this good news. "The time you've been waiting for is here; the Lord has come. He is in your midst." In one sense, the *Gospel* existed before the Gospels; that is, the good news once taught by Jesus was proclaimed by his disciples to Jews and Gentiles long before it was set down in writing.

The Church existed before the Gospels: there was already a community of believers long before the emergence in written form of the four Gospels. The Church was growing and increasing daily in numbers. It was young, spirited, brimming with life and enthusiasm before the Gospels were ever penned. We could say that *the Gospels grew out of the Church*. Preachers and catechists instructed Jewish audiences about the fulfillment of the old covenant promises. Gentiles were being won over by the forthright and persuasive message of Christian missionaries. New communities of Christians were being established in the *diaspora*. Fresh converts proclaimed Jesus as Lord in faraway places — Antioch, Corinth and even Rome. All of this preceded the writing of the Gospels.

Much else was happening. Paul, "still breathing murderous threats against the disciples of the Lord" (Ac 9:1), was knocked to the ground on his way to Damascus, soon to accept Jesus as the Risen Lord. Stephen suffered death at the hands of hostile Jews to become the Church's first martyr. Gentile Christians were arguing with their Jewish colleagues over the relevance of circumcision and dietary regulations, a matter which was to provoke the convocation of the first "council" of Jerusalem around 49-50 A.D. James, the first bishop of Jerusalem was likewise martyred. All of these happenings preceded the writing of the Gospels. The written

Gospel, then, grew out of the life of the Church. Following Jesus of Nazareth and before the time of the Gospels, we have the apostles, the post-apostolic Christian community and ultimately, the evangelists. The final makeup of the Gospels includes, then, the growth and development of the Good News as influenced by the Spirit-filled activity of the early Church.

Present day scholarship takes greater cognizance of the all-important role of this *oral tradition* and its influence on the eventual formulation of the Gospels. Because of contemporary Scripture studies we are better able to appreciate today how the final portrayal of Jesus Christ in the Gospels is the result of a long process, which only gradually evolved into written forms that emerged from the life and practical needs of the early Church.

Earliest Proclamation of the Good News

The earliest Christian preaching proclaimed Jesus as *Lord*. In the face of his shameful death, preachers were saying, "God raised him... and made him Lord" (Ac 2:24, 36). Had his life ended on the hill of Calvary, he may have been mistaken as an ordinary Jewish criminal. But he was raised from the dead! And this made all the difference in the world! He had not abandoned them; he remained with them — but in a radically *new* way.

So, at the heart of the very earliest Christian preaching was the death and resurrection of Jesus. His death was not merely the end of a good man; his resurrection was more than an astonishing sequel to a tragedy. Rather, they said, his death and resurrection had a redeeming value for all those who were willing to accept him and become united with him. "You have been saved by the death and resurrection of Jesus," his apostles exclaimed with bold enthusiasm. Their proclamation ended with a question and an invitation: "Will you believe? Are you willing to totally change your lives in accord with this belief? Will you be baptized?"

Peter's Pentecost sermon in Acts 2 is a good example of early Christian preaching about the meaning of Jesus. After his highly symbolic description of the Pentecost phenomenon, Peter ad-

dressed the audience and his talk included certain highly significant features:

1. The prophecies of old have been fulfilled and a new age
    has dawned with the coming of Jesus the Christ. He is the
    Messiah, the long-awaited one, thus establishing an
    important link with the promises of old (Ac 2:17-21).
2. Jesus died according to the Scriptures (Ac 2:22-23).
3. He was buried and rose again on the third day (Ac 2:24).
4. He is now exalted at the right hand of the Father and
    sends the Holy Spirit as a visible sign of his present glory
    and power (Ac 2:33).
5. There is a final appeal for decision: Repent and accept this
    radically new way of life (Ac 2:38-40).

Such was the *kerygma* — to use the Greek word employed by
St. Paul. It was the very core of the earliest proclamation about
Jesus. The kerygma was the focal point of the early Church's
preaching about the significance of the death and resurrection of
Jesus. The response sought was one of *faith* in Jesus Christ and a
radical change of lifestyle.

In an earlier document, the first letter to the Corinthians,
Paul reminds his listeners of the same basic message which he
himself had officially received and which he, in turn, was passing
on to them. Though shorter than Peter's sermon, it contains the
same significant features:

1. Christ died for our sins in accordance with the Scriptures
    (1 Cor 15:3).
2. He was raised on the third day in accordance with the
    Scriptures (1 Cor 15:4).

We have every reason to believe that Paul's proclamation of
the kerygma was the earliest, circulating in the Church as far back
as 40, and maybe even 36, A.D. according to some scholars.

The kerygma is important because it provides the basic
pattern or framework for all subsequent pictures of Jesus presented by the Gospel writers. Like a skeleton, the kerygma would

have to be "fleshed in" with further details of the life, ministry and teaching of Jesus, and then arranged in a logical, if not strictly chronological, order.

Further reason for the importance of the kerygma existed in the basic unity it provided for all of the Gospels, even for the entire New Testament. No matter how much the evangelists differ in outlook, emphasis or depiction of Jesus, all agree with the kerygma. Mark's realistic and graphic portrayal of Jesus as the suffering Messiah, for example, differs from Matthew's picture of Jesus as the fulfillment of Jewish hopes and expectations. Luke's depiction of Jesus as champion of the poor, outcasts and sinners varies slightly from the first two. In substance, *kerygmatically*, the three are the same: we have all been redeemed through the death and resurrection of Jesus Christ! Here we have the key to the "unity amid diversity" which we discover while reading the individual Gospels. First, however, let us pursue the *oral* development of the Good News.

SIGNIFICANCE OF JESUS' DEATH AND RESURRECTION

With the passage of time, the kerygma, or proclamation of the significance of Jesus' death and resurrection, had to be developed and amplified to meet the demands of prospective converts. One can only be impressed by the open enthusiasm and strong convictions of those first disciples who preached about Jesus and called for a radical change of lifestyle. Yet there was need for further explanation. Those first audiences, though impressed, yearned to know more about this man who rose from the dead. If Jesus were truly the Messiah, why was he executed like a common criminal? Was he indeed greater than Moses? How did he realize the promises made of old to David and his family? What did he mean when he spoke about the Kingdom of God? How did this Kingdom differ from the promises made to Israel of old? What were the signs he performed? What did he say about the law? There were so many other questions to be answered.

Naturally, a need arose, not merely to describe what Jesus had actually said and done, but more important, to explain the meaning and significance of Jesus for the *present*. It was necessary to define the demands his message made of followers in that generation. Clearly, in the first few decades after the departure of Jesus, new situations and circumstances in the early Church required of the disciples of Jesus an explanation of the relevance of the Messiah's words and works.

The entire story of how this oral tradition about Jesus assumed *written* form is not simple history. There is not enough evidence to allow for a clear picture of the actual transition from oral to written Gospel. As helpful as it would have been there is no chapter-by-chapter account of how the Gospels were formed. What is known is learned from an *internal analysis* of the Scriptures themselves.

There are other factors which add to the complexity of the problem. Present-day understanding of authorship does not always appreciate the evolution of oral traditions within a living community. Today's authors, given time and resources, present a finished manuscript to a publisher, who produces and distributes their bound book. The author is solely responsible for the book's content unless a ghost-writer or editor assists. These are generally given credit for their contribution.

The biblical concept of authorship is much broader. It allows for many people to contribute to the final product. Authorship is loosely attributed, even to those responsible for a Gospel's complete edition and final form. The "good news," as we have seen, was basically the *Jesus-event*, which lived and developed and was then transmitted within the living tradition of the early Christian community. Only after a period of growth and maturation did the written Gospels come into being. Such was the work of the evangelists, "authors" only in the broadest sense of the term. The *Jesus-traditions*, his words and works, were not frozen in time. They were not preserved in a library or museum. They were dynamic and alive, preached and confessed. Catechists and preachers utilized these traditions inventively to portray the meaning of Jesus in the lives of their audiences.

Still another factor should be considered. Initially, an atmosphere of expectation developed about the imminent return of Jesus, riding triumphantly on the clouds of heaven to restore his

Kingdom. With some, it reached a high level of expectancy, even anxiety. The first generation of Christians were quite taken with the prophecies of Daniel, interpreting them to mean an imminent coming of the Lord. Indeed, it is precisely this kind of expectation which permeates Paul's first letter to the Thessalonians and which is apparent again in certain portions of Mark's Gospel.

Conversely, there were Christians who were coming to realize that the Lord's return would be, for the present, in the form of the Holy Spirit. They envisioned a more distant future unfolding before them and realized that they might have to prepare for a "long haul," because, when all was said and done, no one knew "the time or the hour." Ultimately, the latter opinion prevailed, so that a formulation of the life and message of Jesus soon became a practical necessity. But in the meantime, three or four decades had already elapsed before the first of the Gospels was recorded.

So then, the core of the Christian message, focusing on the death and resurrection of Jesus and the call for decision and change of life, was gradually expanded to meet new demands, problems, and circumstances within the Christian community. The basic pattern of the kerygma was pieced together and expanded. The result was a literary type which the world had never known before: the *Gospel narrative* about Jesus the Christ.

QUESTIONS FOR DISCUSSION

1. Can the Gospels communicate a historically credible picture of Jesus, even if they are not strict history books or critical biographies?

2. Why did Paul deem it more important to write to his newly-founded communities about the significance of the death and resurrection of Jesus for the Christian life, rather than to describe in detail the life and ministry of Jesus? Which do you consider more important?

3. How do you understand the expression: "The Scriptures are the words of God in human words"?

4. Does the *human* factor in the composition of the Gospels strengthen or weaken your vision of Jesus?

5. If there was a period of almost thirty years when the Jesus-traditions, his words and deeds, were preached before ultimately being recorded, how does this affect the "final picture"?

6. In light of the preaching of the first disciples and mission-aries, what would you consider fundamental for the proclamation of the Christian message today? In your opinion, how is this done most effectively?

7. Are the Christian churches effective in making that message known in our own times?

8. How can lay people best communicate the "good news"?

CHAPTER II

THE GOSPEL: FROM ORAL TO WRITTEN

Matthew 1 - 28

*I*n Chapter One special attention was given to the all-important role of oral tradition in the gradual formation of the Gospels. A few decades had passed between the first proclamation of the Good News and the earliest written accounts. We have seen how the Good News was first preached; how the first preachers emphasized the significance of the death and resurrection; how they called their listeners to faith in Jesus Christ and to a radical conversion of lifestyle.

The Good News was given its basic thrust by Jesus during his public ministry. But after his death, it had to continue; it had to be applied and adapted to the daily life of the post-Easter community and to all of its new problems and circumstances. The Good News was not transmitted in a vacuum, or fostered in a greenhouse. The lived experience of the early Christian community functioned as a filter through which the message of Jesus passed. This message was shaped and molded by a believing people who took for granted that the Jesus who once *was*, had become the Lord who *is*. Now his presence continued in a new form: the abiding presence of the Holy Spirit.

The Gospels which developed subsequently were not the result of a reporter's "on-the-spot coverage" of the life and times of Jesus. They were not researched and compiled within the stuffy enclosures of some academic library. The Good News was dynamic, alive, challenging, decision-provoking — an existential reality in the lives of Jesus' followers. It was the Word, growing and developing within a believing community. This reality gave courage and hope to the members, a truth to live by, a reason for caring and loving others and, most of all, a joyful stance toward the future.

At this point it is important to consider in greater detail the process of development from the oral to the earliest written accounts, giving special emphasis to the shaping and molding process of the early Christian community. Let us always bear in mind, however, the difficulties involved when dealing with living testimonies like the Gospels. While current biblical scholarship has contributed many new tools and techniques for a more critical understanding of the Gospels, the nature of these writings is such that they do not allow for detailed explanations or precise descriptions of each step in the *formative* process.

Fortunately, there are some recent guidelines from the teaching *magisterium* of the Church. In an Instruction from the Biblical Commission entitled "The Historical Truth of the Gospels," issued by Pope Paul VI on April 21, 1964, the entire process of Gospel formation is conveniently broken down into three phases or stages of transmission. Though it may be difficult, if not impossible, to determine precisely where one stage ends and the other begins, there are certain compass points for determining the historical progression of the first three Gospels. In terms of the document, the three stages of tradition through which the words and works of Jesus have come down to us are: 1. Jesus; 2. the apostolic community; and 3. the evangelists.

In its own way, each stage contributed to the final product. Examining each of these stages should give us a better understanding of the formation of the Gospels and how the community slowly deepened in its understanding of Jesus. Gradually, and only after the resurrection, did his followers become aware of who Jesus really was, and what his message truly demanded. Only with the passage of time did they begin adapting his message to new circumstances, with new insights, new concepts, and with a new terminology.

The Gospels, then, were the product of the early Church's

growing and maturing experience of Jesus Christ. A more critical investigation of the text will help us to identify that living experience of the first century. More importantly, it will help us to see why this message has to become part of *our own experience* in the twenty-first century.

The first chapter highlighted the importance of oral tradition and the special significance of the death and resurrection of Jesus in the earliest preaching. It will now help to sketch the entire process *chronologically*, from the earliest stage, beginning with Jesus of Nazareth, and then to show the subsequent influence of the Christian community upon the tradition of Jesus.

JESUS FROM NAZARETH

Jesus taught much like the religious teachers of his time. He was, after all, a *rabbi*, a religious teacher, a "lay theologian" of sorts; an itinerant preacher. His manner of teaching would not have differed radically from his rabbinical counterparts. His repertoire, like theirs, included graphic stories and illustrations mirroring the daily life of first-century Palestine: illustrations and references from the Old Testament, short maxims and proverbial sayings so typical of Eastern sages.

To be sure, Jesus taught with a new "twist." He spoke with far greater authority, arousing admiration among some of his listeners, anger and hostility among others. As far as external form, his general approach and technique were not so different from those of other itinerant religious teachers of the time. He relied exclusively upon the *spoken* word. As far as can be determined, *he* never kept notes or circulated written lessons. There was as yet no need to set his message down in writing.

Like the Jewish teachers of his day, Jesus, too, gathered about himself a group of disciples, intimate associates who accompanied him throughout Galilee and Judea. These were the men "who left all to follow him," who listened intently to his message and remembered his instruction. These men were the chosen witnesses of the many signs Jesus performed, the same who eventually devoted themselves to the continuation of his mission.

The earliest disciples, commonly referred to as "the Twelve," and then the many others who followed, would play a key role in the future dissemination of the Good News.

The close association between Jesus and the disciples during his public ministry made it possible for his message to continue with fidelity and integrity long after his departure from this world. As was seen previously, the first heralds of the Gospel proclaimed Jesus as *Lord*. He who was crucified had risen. His death and resurrection, the disciples insisted, would have vital significance for those who believed. But a change was taking place, a transition from the teaching of Jesus to a proclamation *about* him: the Jesus who taught was now the Messiah who was taught! The "good news" of the Kingdom of God, the hallmark of Jesus' teaching while on earth, was now more profoundly understood as the realm of the *Spirit* made available by the Risen Lord.

The first disciples, teachers, and missionaries continued his basic message. They were faithful to the Master's teaching, though they used other words and concepts. The resurrection and the coming of the Spirit infused them with a vitally new understanding of Jesus, more profound than the one they had known when Jesus was with them on earth. Furthermore, they were now proclaiming the meaning of Jesus as Lord to people living in situations and circumstances never encountered by Jesus. More important than getting back to the very words of Jesus, now the Gospels were becoming a faithful transmission of what these words and expressions *meant* to his followers. Faithful continuity of a person and his message evolved, even when the terms and concepts changed. The Jesus who lived was now proclaimed as the Christ who *lives*... through his Spirit. Pentecost made all the difference in the world!

Some readers of the Gospels are quite surprised, even dismayed, when first hearing about the reformulation of the words of Jesus after his departure. If so, they conclude, we may not have the *exact words* of Jesus. Further questions arise quite naturally: Just how much of his actual message *do* we have? How can we be sure we have his words at all? Is there some chance of distortion or falsification? How can we be certain that those responsible for the Gospels didn't fabricate stories about Jesus?

Exact Words of Jesus

The problem is a modern one. Those responsible for passing on the Jesus-tradition did not have such fears and scruples over exactness of words or detailed description of events. More important for them than the exact reproduction of the Lord's words or a photographic duplication of his works was fidelity to the *meaning* of his words and to the *significance* of his works. Fidelity does not demand exact duplication; faithful transmission of a message does not necessarily mean using the messenger's very same words. Such fidelity is cold and mechanical, rigid and inflexible, hardly adaptable to *new* times and circumstances. Faithful transmission of tradition was not so rigidly understood by the apostolic community and the evangelists. Their word was ever new, ever alive, ever challenging; not by repeating the exact words of Jesus, but by interpreting the significance of those words to the needs and problems of their audiences. To demand exact words and details would be to bind a faithful interpreter in a strait-jacket. Christian churches have always articulated their creeds in terminology quite different from that used by Jesus, simply because new times and circumstances demanded such reformulation. Yet no one challenges their *fidelity*; the *substance* of their message is the same. There is more to be said about the "truth" of "interpreted history." For the moment the role of oral tradition must be emphasized: the Jesus-event was first *preached* for a number of years before it ever was recorded.

With the sophisticated forms of contemporary communication, the immediacy of the print and visual media, it is hard for us to imagine a time when there was *only* the spoken word. Persons and events of the past, even those about whom little is known, can be researched, studied and illumined today through a variety of disciplines. All of this was lacking in first-century Palestine. People at that time had to rely on the power and fidelity of the spoken word. The printing press did not appear until fifteen hundred years later!

The written word was a luxury at the time of Jesus and his companions, restricted to the learned. What happened in the absence of the written word? People communicated by word of mouth; they acquired the art and skill of oral tradition, preserving significant words and events of the past in a remarkable way. It was the *only* way ordinary people could perpetuate precious memories of the past. The Old Testament offers many examples of words spoken by prominent personalities like Moses and some of the prophets which were passed on for decades, even centuries, by word of mouth. Rhythmic speech patterns and poetic line forms were often used to make memorization easier. There would have been nothing unusual about first and second generation followers of Jesus preserving his words with remarkable fidelity. One would expect the followers of the Lord to transmit the message of their beloved Master faithfully, not just "in Jerusalem, but throughout Judea and Samaria, even to the ends of the earth" (Ac 1:8).

There is still another factor to consider when speaking of the faithful transmission of the words of Jesus: the change or reformulation necessitated by a new *language*. More than likely, Jesus spoke in the language used by the people living in and around Galilee and Judea, probably a Palestinian dialect of *Aramaic*. Yet the earliest accounts of his words and deeds are in Greek, the more common written language of that period. Not only a change in language, Greek represents another culture, with different thought patterns and ways of expression. Even when the substance is translated, a certain qualitative change occurs; a nuance, a colloquial expression, is lost in most translations no matter how faithful. Once again, we must emphasize fidelity to the *meaning* of Jesus' message rather than exact verbal duplication.

THE APOSTOLIC COMMUNITY

The second stage of Gospel transmission mentioned in the document of the Biblical Commission is that of the apostolic community. This stage refers to the first generation Christians, especially the disciples who were eye-witnesses to the events of Jesus' life, and those who, like the apostles, continued to preach the essentials of the "good news" after his death. They were responsible for spreading the Gospel by word of mouth from approximately 33 A.D. until it was completed in written form by the evangelists. These disciples spread the Word quickly and widely. They accommodated themselves to the practical necessities of their audiences, which arose from worship, catechetical instruction of potential converts, apostolic controversies with Jewish antagonists and from inquiries regarding standards of discipleship. In so doing, they did not merely repeat the words and works of Jesus, but interpreted them according to the particular needs of their audiences. At times it was found advantageous to rephrase sayings, recast and reformulate transmitted stories and then, finally, to link them together and arrange them for catechetical or preaching purposes.

The very practical necessities of the apostolic community influenced the shape and form of the Jesus-material as it was communicated to the people. A gradual reshaping and molding process began, like a pebble worn down by a moving stream. From constant repetition, the oral traditions about Jesus assumed a certain stereotypical form, their rough edges smoothed away and polished. What is more, they grew into isolated, self-contained units without any specific geographical framework or time setting. Take for example an oft-quoted expression like: "Ask not what your country can do for you, but ask what you can do for your country." When and where this pithy statement was first used by President John F. Kennedy is not usually known. (It was used by him in his Inaugural Address, Jan. 20, 1961.) But many subsequent speakers have borrowed that famous phrase and used it as the situation demanded.

The Gospels, too, have examples of short, crisp sayings of Jesus, "one-liners," which have been given an illustrative quality, but only for the purpose of serving as punch lines for a story. To cite a few: "People who are healthy do not need a doctor; sick people do." / "I have come to call sinners, not the self-righteous." / "The Sabbath was made for man, not man for the Sabbath." / "Give to Caesar what is Caesar's, but give to God what is God's." Each of these sayings, while undoubtedly originating with Jesus, has been placed into a new context. The story or the framework exists merely to convey the message. Such bywords illustrated or illumined some of the nitty-gritty problems or questions that faced Christians in their individual or corporate lives, e.g.: Do we have to pay taxes? Must we follow the many detailed laws prescribed for the Sabbath? What attitude should we take toward outcasts and sinners? While Jesus' original context may have been forgotten, the teaching was not; it was simply inserted into a new context according to the circumstances.

Another example of the reshaping process caused by frequent repetition is evident in the "miracle episodes." Nearly all of the miracle accounts have the same basic four-step format: request for a cure or favor, demand for faith, the miracle itself, audience reaction. While catechists and missionaries who used the miracle stories found it easier to remember and retell them by following a certain pattern, they often altered the *form* of the episode. More important than form, however, was fidelity to the *substance* of the miracle.

In fact, the four-step pattern common to Gospel miracle accounts tended to emphasize the third step, the demand for faith. The actual description of the miracle itself was often toned down. One could read with profit the miracle narratives found in Matthew's Gospel (8 and 9), paying special attention to the accent given to the dialogue, especially the demand for faith. The actual miracle appears to be given secondary importance, very much in contrast with the extra-biblical miracle accounts of the time which highlighted the extraordinary and bizarre aspects of such events.

It now becomes clear what was taking place. The apostolic community was showing a certain flexibility and freedom in transforming the Jesus-traditions to fit the needs of their audience. They had no qualms about reformulating the words of Jesus, and rewording the events of his life. They were, after all, faithful to their Master by presenting the significance of his message for people *now*, that is, living in *their* own generation. When we read the Gospels today, we must remember that we are not reading the exact words of Jesus in his own life setting, but of Jesus Christ, the Risen Lord, speaking through his Holy Spirit to the life situation of the post-Easter Christian community.

Gospels Influenced by Community Needs

The Jesus-material was being shaped and molded by the living context of the early Church. But how? What were the specific situations or life settings which influenced that style of presentation? There is general agreement among Scripture scholars on three such sources of influence: *Liturgical Celebration, Catechetical Instruction* and *Missionary Preaching*. Even if an exact reconstruction is not possible due to lack of concrete evidence, there certainly is material enough for a general sketch.

Liturgical Celebration

Soon after the departure of Jesus, his followers came together to "break bread," an early expression for eucharistic celebrations. At the outset of the rite, a community leader, generally an apostle, would recount some key event from the life of Jesus, or he would recall significant words: how Jesus came to be crucified, what he said about the Law, his concern for outcasts and sinners, or whatever aspect was especially applicable to them. It resembled somewhat the first part of the Mass, the liturgy of the Word, though the context was far more informal. After all, the setting was that of a meal.

Although clear-cut evidence is lacking, it may have been precisely such a liturgical context which provided the opportunity for the apostles and others to elaborate in greater detail the entire story of the crucifixion: how Jesus was betrayed by one of his own, his words at the Last Supper, how he submitted himself freely to his captors to fulfill the prophecies of the Isaian "Suffering Servant," how God's love for all was realized in the sacrificial death of his Son, the attitude of the Jewish religious authorities, the reaction of the crowds. In those first decades after the departure of the Lord, the crucifixion would have been an important topic, because for potential Jewish converts there was always that gnawing question: "If Jesus were indeed the Messiah, why was he crucified?" Some scholars feel that the Passion narratives may have originated in such liturgical contexts. Recounted in detail, shaped and formed by constant repetition, and finally written down, these narratives were probably one of the earliest oral accounts to be so composed.

Another instance of liturgical influence appears in the Last Supper accounts. Jesus' words over the bread and wine reflect the liturgical formulas used in the eucharistic celebrations of Jerusalem (Mt and Mk) and Antioch (Lk and 1 Cor 11), rather than the exact words Jesus himself pronounced at the Last Supper. Substantially they are the same, but the formulaic pattern, rhythm and terseness of wording reflect more of a liturgical formula than the actual spoken words of Jesus at a meal. As a matter of fact, the same eucharistic formulas may have influenced the miracle accounts of the multiplication of loaves where Jesus "blessed bread, broke, and gave it to his disciples" (Mt 14:19; cf. also Mk 6:41; Lk 9:16 and Mt 26:26; Mk 14:22 and Lk 22:19). No one felt scrupulous that the exact words of Jesus were not being used. More important, they were being faithful to what Jesus had done and to its significance.

Catechetical Instruction

More influential than the liturgy was the catechetical instruction given by the early Church. Before conversion to Christianity, candidates had to learn the main features of Jesus' life and the principal tenets of his message. For converts from Judaism especially, steeped as they were in the hope and promises of the Old Testament, the need to convey the significance of Jesus in terms of his fulfillment of those promises was prominent. "Was Jesus the Messiah?" they would ask. "And if so, how?" "Would he restore Israel to that position of privilege and power it once enjoyed and to which it was destined in the future?" Like good catechists knowing their audiences, they spoke of Jesus in concepts taken from the Old Testament, thus accommodating themselves to the religious needs and deep-seated longings of their Jewish brothers and sisters. What they knew of his life, they explained in terms of fulfillment of the Scriptures.

The infancy narratives of Matthew, for example, are by no means an exact factual presentation of the birth and early childhood of Jesus, but they are a tissue of allusions from the Old Testament intended to bear out the special significance of the birth of the Messiah. A closer reading of Matthew's text (chapters 1 and 2) reveals the special emphasis given to the fulfillment of the Scriptures in the birth of the infant Jesus (cf. 1:23; 2:6; 2:15; 2:18; 2:23). He was indeed the Messiah, and he did fulfill, as no one before him, the words of the Torah and the Prophets.

The third Gospel, on the other hand, is directed primarily to the Gentiles. Luke uses the same material, though he slants it differently. Throughout the Gospel, he shows Jesus' deep concern for the poor, the outcasts and sinners, an attitude more consistent with the circumstances of non-Jews. In Luke's depiction of the birth of Jesus, while fulfillment themes are not absent, he portrays Jesus as "wrapped in swaddling clothes" (the raiment of the poor!) and "lying in a manger, because there was no room for them in the inn" (Lk 2:7). He was visited, not by prominent astrologers from the East, but by simple shepherds. But no one says there is any contradiction between the Jesus presented by Luke and that portrayed by Matthew. As good catechists and apologists, the two evangelists used the traditions about the birth of Jesus differently, better to suit the needs of their varied audiences.

Another example of creative catechetical adaptation is the dramatic illustration of the temptation of Jesus as recounted in Mt 4:1-11 and Lk 4:1-13. What did the Gospel writers actually know of the spiritual experience of Jesus' temptations? Only that the crowds wanted him to be a popular, political Messiah, while he was unwilling to project such an image. With the actual depiction of such an experience, the accounts of the temptation were "dressed up" by contrasting them with the temptations of Israel in the desert as recorded in the Pentateuch.

Jesus thus became the personification of Israel. As the Israel of old was tempted three times in the desert and succumbed, so the "new Israel," Jesus, was also tempted. But he did not succumb. He was proven obedient. Jesus, the "new Israel," accomplished what the old Israel could not; he remained true to his calling. No one was upset that perhaps it didn't "happen" exactly that way. In truth,

Jesus fulfilled his vocation, even to the point of an ignominious death. He did not yield to the popular idols placed before him as Israel of old had done. He remained true to his Father's will.

Similar things could be said regarding the accounts of the baptism of Jesus, his transfiguration, his appearances after the resurrection. The details and wording of a story were frequently adjusted to bring home the significance of a certain truth, without ever intending to mislead or deceive the hearer or reader. In fact, almost every page of the Gospels bears some trace of the influence of catechetical instruction.

Missionary Preaching

The third influence on the formation of the Gospel tradition was the need for missionary preaching to those who had never actually seen or heard Jesus. Here we might single out the miracle stories once again. Jesus gave witness to the validity of his mission by performing numerous signs and acts of power generally referred to as *miracles*. Primarily, the miracles serve to offer graphic demonstration of the arrival of God's Kingdom. The presence of God's Kingdom was marked by a conflict with the powers of chaos and disorder. All forms of disorder, physical or moral, were now being overcome; the kingdom of evil was being supplanted by a new reality of order and healing. We shall discuss miracles at greater length in a later chapter.

For the present, let us simply highlight the apologetic aspect of the miracles. Naturally, the first missionaries were intent on convincing their listeners that Jesus was the Messiah, the Son of God, that he did really introduce the long-awaited messianic age. What more effective way of doing this than to highlight the many wondrous cures and healings that were performed by Jesus during his lifetime? Were these signs not comparable to those performed by God's emissaries in the Old Testament?

As one might expect of effective preachers, however, they presented their audiences with more than a bland, colorless enumeration of miracles performed by Jesus. The sign and wonder traditions which they had received were hardly passed on like items on a grocery list! Dressed up, and frequently placed into a graphic narrative context, early Christian preachers placed a great deal of emphasis on the dialogue between the recipient of the miracle and Jesus. The reaction of onlookers was often drama-tized. They utilized a bit of "narrative license" to convey the meaning of the miracles to convince others that Jesus was, indeed, the anointed one whom God had sent.

A brief comparison of some miracle accounts will reveal how they differ from each other in content, form and position. To cite an example: if you compare the miracle stories of Matthew 8 and 9 with their parallel sections in Mark and Luke, many interesting variations begin to appear. For example, compare: Mt 8:28-34 with Mk 5:1-20 and Lk 8:26-39; also Mt 9:18-26 with Mk 5:21-43 and Lk 8:40-56.

As far as content, Matthew downplays the prodigious or wondrous aspects of a miraculous account and concentrates on the demand for faith, especially in the dialogue between Jesus and the beneficiary of the miracle. One receives the distinct impression that Matthew considers the dialogue about faith as more impor-tant than the miracle itself. A prior faith was always asked of the petitioner, implicitly or explicitly. For Matthew's audiences, who had never really seen Jesus, the insistence on faith was a very important element. As zealous missionaries, the evangelists were not only concerned with recounting the miraculous event itself, but they also wanted to communicate the faith response of the miracle's beneficiary in the hope of drawing a similar response from their listeners.

Sometimes miracle accounts were arranged or positioned in such a way that the theological intention stands out with promi-nence. A good example appears in the first three miracles stories in Matthew 8:1-17, where we witness the healing of a Jew, a pagan's servant, and Peter's mother-in-law. More than likely, the chronological arrangement is not original to the miracles. But it does not matter. Far more important is the theological intention of Matthew: Jesus has come to assume the burdens and sufferings of all people. What could be more mission-minded? The love of God for all makes no distinctions of race, religion, or social standing.

Worship, catechetical instruction and missionary preaching

each influenced the way the Gospel stories were expressed and the way they were grouped together. The early preachers were not interested in presenting cold, factual descriptions of all that Jesus had said and done. More vital was the significance of these happenings to their audiences. Their aim was also "existential." They were interpreting the *meaning* of Jesus.

Had they presented their contemporaries with bare-boned factual descriptions of the Jesus event, as accurate as that picture may have been, it would never have evoked a faith response. A portrayal of Jesus, colored by their own personal convictions that Jesus was Lord and Messiah, gave their hearers a living, dynamic word. They told it like it was and obviously really meant it! This was a word that was attractive, hopeful, yet challenging. This was the "Good News" of Jesus Christ.

Questions for Discussion

1. Is your image of Jesus that of an "itinerant preacher"? Religious teacher? How do you visualize him?

2. Just how important is it for believers today to know the "exact words" of Jesus?

3. What is the difference between the preaching about Jesus by the first disciples, and that of a priest today preaching on the Gospel text?

4. Does the Christian in today's community have any influence on the communication of the "good news"?

5. When the words of Jesus were filtered through the life of the Christian community, did they still remain the genuine words of Jesus? What determines the genuine, true and faithful transmission of God's word in our own times?

6. What lessons may be learned for contemporary catechesis from the way the apostolic community conveyed the significance of Jesus' words and deeds?

7. What do you consider the most effective technique for conveying the significance of Jesus' message today? How successful has it been?

CHAPTER III

THE EVANGELISTS

Luke 1 - 24

The third and last stage mentioned in the document from the Biblical Commission, "The Historical Truth of the Gospels," concerns the role of the evangelists: Matthew, Mark, Luke and John. Their work is the logical and chronological outgrowth of the two previous stages, those of Jesus and of the apostolic community, thus completing the process of Gospel formation. The previous stages showed how the oral traditions about Jesus were shaped and influenced by the post-Easter Church's practical necessities. The final stage highlights the role of the individual persons, the evangelists.

Groups of people are not generally known to be responsible for any final written product, though no one would deny a certain group influence on the circulating traditions about Jesus. The audiences of the Globe Theatre, for example, were not responsible for writing Shakespeare's plays. Nor would anyone say that *Das Kapital* was the expression of the frustrations and deep yearnings of the poorer class for a better society. If not for the untiring zeal and literary efforts of a bearded old man by the name of Karl Marx, who labored for many years in the British Museum, gathering together, arranging, and then formulating those yearnings into a coherent ideology, there might never have been a basic constitution for Marxism. Similarly, the Gospels, although very much influenced in form by a living community, required the dedication of certain individuals to pull all of the variant traditions together into a unified composition. Such was the role of the evangelists.

We already have some idea of the slow, gradual process involved in the formation of the Gospels. The Good News originated with Jesus. After his death and resurrection, the spoken traditions of his words and works were passed on, utilized, applied and interpreted according to the practical necessities of the apostolic community. The Jesus-event was still very much alive; it was proclaimed enthusiastically and not frozen in written form. It was not a biography, a chronicle of Jesus' life and works, or a catechism passed around to potential converts. The Good News was living testimony serving the practical necessities of the nascent Christian community which began to confront new crises and situations not present during the lifetime of Jesus.

With the passage of time, the avid expectation of the Lord's impending return and the restoration of his Kingdom began to wane. There was still that note of urgency and eager expectation in Paul's first letter to the Thessalonians, written as early as 51 A.D. By the time of Mark's Gospel, though, even while an air of expectation still remained, the idea began to fade. At this juncture, the Gospel tradition prepares for the "long haul." Provision for the future would have to be made if the mission of Jesus was to continue. Now it would be necessary to set down *in writing* the words and works of Jesus.

There were other substantial reasons as well. The mounting success of the Gentile mission necessitated written catechetical material for preachers and missionaries who had not witnessed Jesus personally. Controversy with Jewish religious authorities in an atmosphere of open hostility demanded the formulation of Jesus' sayings about the role of Israel. Disciplinary and organizational problems within the burgeoning community prompted the recall of Jesus' words and the application of his commands to the disciples. Questions were being asked about the essentials of discipleship: what responsibilities did the disciple have to unbelievers, to unconverted Jews, to fellow Christians, to the Roman state?

There was also the danger of heresy. As Christianity expanded rapidly beyond the boundaries of Palestine to the very

heart of the Roman Empire, teachings at variance with that of
Jesus and the apostolic leaders began to appear on the scene. Who
would be able to determine the authenticity of a given saying of
Jesus, or of a certain teaching, when the first, and even second,
generation disciples were dying off? There were no official dogmas
or normative procedures as yet to bind Christians together as one
community. Questions naturally began to arise; the responses
were not always uniform. Did Jesus really suffer and die, or was
he some kind of heavenly creature, merely clothed in a material
body? If he really suffered and died, how was he divine? Was he
only a man, unique and extraordinary to be sure, but a man like
any other? It was high time for someone to set down in writing a
faithful and official record of the words and works of Jesus, what
they meant to his followers, their significance for potential converts.

It was inevitable that someone would start collecting the
various traditions (most of them still oral, other smaller units
already in written form) and begin compiling and editing them
into a unified, cohesive account. Such was the work of the
evangelists, those who left a final and lasting imprint on the Gospel
traditions.

There is good reason to believe that the compositional
process worked backwards: what came last *chronologically*, the
death of Jesus, was the first to be written down. An internal
analysis of the narrative accounts will reveal that the events
surrounding Jesus' passion and death were recorded quite early.
It is difficult to ascribe any precise date because of the nature of
the sources. Perhaps they originated in the context of liturgical
gatherings when the subject of Jesus' death was explained in more
detail by the apostolic leaders. Allusion has been made to this view
in the previous chapter. One contemporary scholar refers to
Mark's Gospel as a "passion narrative with an introduction."

Other major events followed, but in reverse order: (1) the
journey to Jerusalem and the events preceding the trial, passion
and death; (2) the public ministry of Jesus in Galilee; and (3) what
is for us the beginning of the Gospel, the preparatory stage of John
the Baptist and the initial preaching by Jesus of the Kingdom of
God. Into this framework the evangelists arranged the sayings of

Jesus and the narratives depicting the events of his life, depending on their own special compositional and theological designs.

That there was a certain selectivity from among the many traditions available becomes clear with a statement found in John's Gospel: "Jesus also did many other signs in the presence of the disciples, which are not written in this book, but these things have been written so you may believe that Jesus is the Messiah, the Son of God, and so that by believing, you may have life in his name" (Jn 20:30-31).

The evangelists not only chose from among the many traditions available, but also arranged and organized these into a logical sequence, abbreviating, expanding or even transposing where necessary. With further diligence, the evangelists then grouped these selections into larger complexes, "stitched" them together, and interpreted the Gospel accounts one last time to suit the needs of their audiences. Thus the finished Gospel product as we now have it came into being. The evangelists were not concerned with telling everything, only that which would help the reader to "believe that Jesus is the Messiah, the Son of God." The first three Gospels, then, are like three separate mosaics of Jesus. The image is the same, but the choice, variety and final arrangement of the pieces lies in the artistry, design and theological motivation of each evangelist.

AUTHOR(S) OF THE GOSPELS?

Matthew, Mark and Luke are not just compilers or editors of previously existing material. Their conclusive work on the Gospels has earned for them the title "authors," although such authorship must be understood as broadly as possible — at least by modern standards. They alone were not responsible for the final product. The Gospels, remember, are said to be "according to" Matthew, Mark, Luke and John. They were the ones who wove all of the traditions together and imparted the final design to the finished product.

God, in the person of Jesus Christ, is the ultimate author of the Gospels, insofar as he is the source or basis for the words and deeds recounted. The evangelists are the "authors" of the Gospels because they gave the living traditions their final stamp, leaving for posterity the written Gospels as we know them today. Divinity and humanity contributed to the final product, each in different ways.

AUTHORSHIP AND INSPIRATION

Before we consider the slightly different portraits of the same Jesus Christ, as presented by the first three evangelists, it may be helpful to consider briefly the broadened notion of authorship in relation to the concept of *inspiration*.

From what has been discussed about the complex nature of Gospel authorship, it becomes apparent that the "author" of a Gospel was not just one individual, an inspired writer, singularly endowed with the Holy Spirit who sat down on a given occasion and penned the memoirs of Jesus of Nazareth. Nothing could be farther from the truth, for as has already been suggested, many persons were involved. One would have to say that the entire Christian community of the mid-first century was, in a certain sense, involved in the process.

To limit the prompting of the Holy Spirit to one person alone, an evangelist, would greatly impoverish the notion of inspiration. Without sufficiently comprehending the communal and social dimensions, a resultant understanding of inspiration would be narrow indeed. The Gospels' gradual development from spoken to written stages was a dynamic, Spirit-filled venture, incorporating many different lives and personalities, some of whom history will never remember. Important as they are, the evangelists were not the sole beneficiaries of the gift of inspiration. We must take into account the Pentecost experience, a Spirit-filled community, and the preaching and witness of Spirit-endowed disciples.

The *entire* process of Gospel formation, from beginning to end, with the many different personalities involved, was under the influence of the Holy Spirit. The first disciples of Jesus, the early preachers, catechists, missionaries, evangelists and countless others, may have been involved in the process in diverse ways and to various degrees until the final written form was realized. The ongoing mission of Jesus Christ, indeed his very presence, continued after his death and resurrection in and through the abiding influence of the Holy Spirit. The seminal traditions preached by Jesus grew and matured within the living ambience of a Spirit-filled community. Without the Spirit, there would be no Church, no Sacraments, no written Gospels. Many people responded to the prompting of the Holy Spirit and are, therefore, truly "authors." In former times, however, when the complexity of the Gospel formation process was seen in a more simplified perspective, inspiration was generally attributed to the evangelists alone as the "authors" of the Gospels.

It may be difficult today for us to appreciate and recognize the presence of the Holy Spirit in the lived experience of the early Church, in the faithful witness to the Word as it emerged from people's day-to-day relationships with one another. Perhaps we believe too little and not really well. Like the unbelievers of the Gospels, we also look for irrefutable signs, splashy manifestations, revelations from "on high" to ascertain the presence of the Spirit. Similar to the doubtful Thomas, we may be inclined to say, even to ourselves, "Unless I see, I will not believe." We demand proof. But ordinary experiences of the Holy Spirit, whether in our own times or in those of Jesus, were not spectacular manifestations. As Elijah experienced the Word of the Lord at Horeb "not in howling winds, nor earthquakes, nor in fires, but in a tiny whispering sound" (1 K 19:12), so also the many responsible for the formation and final composition of the Gospels listened to and responded to the tiny whisper of the Spirit.

To summarize: the lived experience of the early Christian community was like a filter through which the "Good News" was passed. It was shaped and molded by a believing community and finally collected, arranged and interpreted by the evangelists. All accepted unquestionably that Jesus who once *was*, became the Lord who *is*, the difference being that now his presence continued in the works of the Spirit.

The evangelists left their own particular brand or stamp on the Gospel material. In this sense they were the Gospels' final interpreters and quite legitimately "authors." They adapted the

Jesus-traditions with a certain freedom and flexibility, and so might also be considered "theologians." They tried to make the Jesus-event relevant to their audiences, which in the case of Matthew and Luke must have been fifty years or more after Jesus' lifetime. Doing otherwise would have risked relegating Jesus, as a person and an event, to ancient history, to the first three decades of the first century A.D. These writers had no intention, however, of "preserving" the Lord as a relic of the past, a museum piece. The evangelists, instead, wished to convey the experience of a *living* God, continually abiding with his people. They testified not merely to the Jesus of yesterday, but to the Lord who says today and all days, "Know that I am with you always, until the end of the world."

The Evangelists Taken Individually

Mark

We know from what has been said already that each evangelist presented his own distinctive picture of Jesus. The first such composition of the Good News was that "according to Mark" (about 65 A.D.), almost thirty-five years after the death and resurrection of Jesus. The first words of Mark's Gospel are: "The beginning of the gospel of Jesus Christ, the Son of God" (Mk 1:11). Mark did not simply want to record the memory of Jesus' ministry. He wanted his account to be an address, a proclamation that would "re-present" Jesus, one that would, in a certain sense, make him available once again. Mark was saying, in effect: Listen! This is how Jesus Christ showed that he was the Son of God. This is the good news which I am going to tell you, and which Jesus himself proclaimed to you.

There was also an implied invitation to this proclamation: If you open your heart and accept in faith this Jesus as Lord, and if you are willing to change your life accordingly, then you will be saved.

Mark's distinctive handling of the material leaves one with a picture of Jesus as the suffering Messiah who is met with

continual disbelief by the general public, even by his own disciples. Mark underscores the people's lack of understanding and
their inability to believe, even after Jesus revealed himself to them
with so many signs. Only after the passion and resurrection does
Jesus finally emerge victorious. The suffering Messiah triumphs
over every form and shape of evil: ignorance, unbelief, pride,
hardness of heart. Such is the "good news" of Mark's Gospel. The
implication is: If you want to be his follower, you too will meet
misunderstanding and rejection on all sides. Yet if you press on
with true faith, you too will overcome.

Matthew

Matthew and Luke, on the other hand, wrote almost twenty
years later (perhaps 85 A.D. or even later) and drew upon Mark
and other available traditions, offering their own interpretations
of Jesus. As might be expected of competent interpreters and
theologians, their depictions of Jesus were suited to the particular
needs of their audiences.

Matthew's Gospel was directed toward Jewish Christians; it
was occasionally referred to as the "Jewish Gospel." It was very
important for new converts from Judaism to recognize in the
person of Jesus Christ the fulfillment of the promises made to their
forefathers of the first covenant. A frequently used formula in
Matthew's Gospel is "... that it may be fulfilled." He makes more
use of the Old Testament in his portrayal of Jesus than do the other
two evangelists. A recurrent theme in Matthew's Gospel is: Jesus
as the Son of God and the Son of David, the Messiah of Judaism.
The "Jewishness" of Matthew's Gospel is apparent in content, and
in its structural arrangement as well. The Gospel appears to be
arranged in five books, each containing a discourse preceded by
a narrative section. What makes this arrangement so attractive
and credible is the possibility that Matthew deliberately structured this Gospel according to a five-book pattern, imitating the
five books of Moses, the "Torah" or "Law" of Judaism. The
evangelist wanted to depict Jesus as a "new Moses," initiating a
"new Torah" and a new understanding of the Law. Such a
recasting of Jesus in Old Testament terms is consistent with a

significant statement attributed to Jesus: "Don't think that I came to destroy the Torah and the Prophets. I came, not to destroy, but to fulfill" (Mt 5:17).

The evangelist was certainly aware that Jesus' life did not develop according to the five-fold pattern of his Gospel. This did not matter. Matthew was more interested in stressing the significance of Jesus as the new Moses who came to initiate a new attitude toward the Law. What could be more effective than communicating an image of Jesus that Jewish Christians could respond to with their deepest longings and sensitivities? Such a Jesus followed in the traditions of their forefathers, and yet he was unlike them. Here lies the difference between Judaism and Christianity.

Furthermore, the writer of the first Gospel, whom we know as Matthew, was not a simple, uneducated disciple but a capable theologian. His skillful casting of Jesus in terms of the Old Testament "fulfillment" theme, and his elaborately structured composition reflects the mind of someone who thought deeply about the meaning of the Lord, and had the ability to formulate it with literary artistry.

The intricate construction of the Gospel according to Matthew leads one to believe that the final composition cannot be attributed to the Matthew who was one of the original Twelve chosen by Jesus. The Gospel is too complex from a literary and theological standpoint to be the work of an uneducated fisherman. Even if this Matthew were a tax collector, as is popularly assumed, he would have been a most unusual one. The author appears to be a highly creative theologian possessing a refined literary style. For this reason, it is quite likely that Matthew, one of the original disciples of Jesus, had little to do with the final formulation of the Gospel which now bears his name. Quite probably, with the passage of time, the first Gospel was attributed to Matthew because his name lent a certain prestige and gave the book a seal of apostolic authority. But others, perhaps the disciples of Matthew, were probably responsible for its final formulation.

Luke

Luke, the author of the third Gospel, has the reputation of being the group's "historian." His purpose was to trace the history of God's plan from the coming of Jesus until the time when the Gospel was preached to the ends of the earth. Actually he is more a theologian of history. He is not scrupulous and exacting in giving the dates and places of the events he records, although he is quite capable of doing so when the context calls for it. Luke was more anxious to present a theological interpretation of events than to write a detailed chronological biography of Jesus. Unlike Matthew and Mark, who thought of history as divided into two periods, one of promise and one of fulfillment, Luke envisaged history as divided into three periods: the time of Israel, the time of Jesus, and the time of the Church.

The time of Jesus is the center of time; it is the time which gives meaning to all of history. Luke is writing from the time period of the Church. He looks back upon the center of time, the period of Jesus, as that which explains the amazing vitality of the Word and the rapid expansion of Christianity. Luke wants to convince his Gentile readers that the obvious manifestations of the Spirit, which they are currently experiencing, are attributable to Jesus, a prophet and a Spirit-filled person himself from the very beginning. Luke has recast and arranged his material in patterns of the three historical periods and interpreted his traditions in such ways that Jesus, born of the Spirit, anointed and commissioned by that Spirit to go out to all, is also the same Jesus Christ so apparent through the Spirit in the community of his time. For this reason, contemporary scholarship has shown that Luke's Gospel and the Acts of the Apostles should be viewed together. They are simply two parts of the same work: Luke-Acts. Through the Holy Spirit, Luke shows the inner unity of salvation history, destined to embrace all nations, Jewish and Gentile alike. The center of his history is always Jesus of Nazareth, Lord of history, present through the activity of the Spirit.

With this third stage of development, the work of the evangelists, the Gospel tradition, becomes fixed. Its verbal development has terminated. It has been and it will ever remain normative for Christianity. We can see why there are basic similarities in the first three Gospels, as well as obvious differences. For this reason, too, the first three Gospels are called the "Synoptic Gospels," because when placed side by side in parallel columns there are such striking resemblances ("Synoptic" comes from the Greek word *syn-ophthein* meaning "to view together"). Yet, because of the interpretative work of the evangelists, there are also equally striking differences.

IMPLICATIONS FOR TODAY'S READER OF THE GOSPELS

The Gospels are not biographies or detailed histories of Jesus. The traditions about Jesus have been so prismed through the life and faith of the early Christian community that a "life of Jesus," unlike an account of the life of Napoleon or Mahatma Gandhi or Abraham Lincoln, would be impossible. The Gospel writers were not interested in a detailed, factual life of Jesus as we might be. They were concerned with telling us what Jesus could *mean* for us, what *significance* he might have for us. Chronological data, geographical and topographical minutiae, accuracy of detail, so important to contemporary historians, play a secondary role in the Gospels. The import of Jesus and his message is primary.

The Gospels do not give us pure history, as for example in Morrison's *Naval History of the Second World War*. The Gospels are "interpreted history," seen through the eyes of the early Christian community. Their historical facts are wedded to an interpretation based on faith in Jesus as Lord, Messiah, Son of God. The Gospel writers are obviously prejudiced in favor of Jesus; they are convinced that he can show the way to the Father, and they are intent on showing us how to follow this way.

When we say we do not have a "detailed history," it does not mean that the Gospels have been fabricated. They are not the product of the creative ingenuity of the early Christian community. They are not a distortion of history. The portrayal of Jesus is no more distorted from historical reality than is a picture of Napoleon, Gandhi or Abraham Lincoln. All of the Gospels are interpreted to some extent, but not so grossly as to lack all basis in historical reality. In every historical account *some* interpretation is inevitable as there is a human factor involved in the very writing of the history. Interestingly, no matter how severe and analytical Gospel criticism tends to be, it never destroys the historical person. At the core of the Gospel account remains a real, credible person, one who has been seen through the eyes of a believing community guided by the Holy Spirit.

The Gospels, in the fullest sense of the word, are confessional testimonies *of* believers *for* believers. They tell us: "We have believed, and we invite you also to believe." Those responsible for the Gospels have taken the risk, made the leap of faith, and reflected back on Jesus, relating to their own readers why it is reasonable and important for them to make that same leap. They have accepted Jesus as Lord, and their account has been interpreted accordingly. Very simply: the evangelists are giving us their own personal testimony to the person of Jesus Christ. In their own faltering, human way the Gospel writers express a profound faith experience, a way of life, an attitude toward people, a vision toward the future, an outlook on life and death, all founded on the person of Jesus Christ.

To approach the Gospels of Jesus Christ, to share in that same experience and to encounter that same Lord as did those first believers, one must approach the text with faith. As the Gospels have been interpreted and written with the eyes of faith, the accounts can be vitally experienced only through the eyes of faith. No amount of sophisticated critical analysis, no purely rational dissection of the text, no matter how brilliant, will yield the true meaning and vital significance of Jesus Christ, without the reader's own faith in the liberating potential of the Word.

To try and prove the history of the Gospels first, and only then to accept Jesus as Son of God is impossible. History and interpretation are so closely wed that one arrives ultimately at a point where critical analysis must yield to the inevitable leap. "I've gone as far as I can go, Lord. I believe, but help my unbelief."

The presence of the Risen Lord, profoundly experienced by the Gospel writers convinces us that the Jesus who speaks now in his Word is the Jesus who spoke during his earthly ministry. For the evangelists, he is one and the same. The manner of speaking about him may vary, but the reality is the same. The Jesus of Mark's Gospel is the Jesus of Mark's Christian experience. The same can be said for Matthew and Luke, and more so for John, writing toward the end of the first century A.D.

Questions for Discussion

1. Is the communication of God's Word in our own times influenced by contemporary crises and problems? Can you give some examples?

2. Does the process of inspiration, seen as the influence of the Holy Spirit upon the many different personalities involved in forming and shaping the Gospels, seem credible? Realistic?

3. Discuss the role of the evangelists as "authors" of the Gospels.

4. Has your own reading of the Gospels revealed other distinctive features of Jesus proper to the first three evangelists? Which of these means more to you personally?

5. In what sense were the evangelists "theologians"? Must one be a theologian in order to communicate the significance and meaning of Jesus in our own times?

6. When you hear the Word of the Lord proclaimed today, do you recognize an implicit invitation: "I have believed and I also invite you to believe in Jesus Christ"?

7. When God's Word is proclaimed, is the reality of the Lord's presence and significance also conveyed? What is lacking in the contemporary preaching of the "good news"?

8. From your personal experience, what are the most effective means for communicating the present reality of Jesus Christ?

Chapter IV

THE KINGDOM OF GOD

Mark 1:1-45; Matthew 3 - 4; 11:2-15; Luke 3 - 4

*F*or most of us who hear the Gospel in snatches and pieces at Mass on Sunday morning, a central unifying theme is not always apparent. We are all familiar with certain sayings of Jesus, the beatitudes, parables, miracle accounts, passages taken from the passion narratives, etc. But is there any one central idea that ties everything together? Is there a dominant theme, a pervading idea, a key feature of Jesus' teaching that stands out above all the others? *Yes!*

The *one* concept that underlies the whole of the New Testament revelation is that of the *Kingdom of God.* Among biblical scholars there is general agreement that the central teaching of Jesus as recorded in the Gospels focuses on this one theme.

The term "Kingdom of God" (more frequently "Kingdom of Heaven" in Matthew) is most common in the Synoptic Gospels. Of the more than 100 times it is found in the New Testament, it appears 70 times in the first three Gospels. More than likely, the reason for its relative infrequency in the rest of the New Testament is the strong Jewish coloring of the term, making it unintelligible to non-Jews, and probably just as puzzling for readers today. At least the early disciples recognized the term as a special theme of Jesus.

As we shall see later, the concept of the Kingdom of God is so central to the teaching of Jesus that without it we cannot fully understand his miracles or parables, nor even the full implications of his call to discipleship. Knowing Jesus Christ is intimately involved with understanding the nature of the Kingdom of God and, above all, living by its demands.

Background of the Kingdom of God Concept

For most of us, "Kingdom of God" is a strange-sounding expression. The very idea of kings is somewhat quaint. Most of us have probably never seen a real king, except perhaps in the movies or on the television screen. We live in no kingdom, and since the separation of our sovereign and independent United States from Great Britain, the experience of living under a king has been relegated to the memory of a bygone age.

When we talk of a biblical understanding of the Kingdom of God, we are twenty centuries removed from a concept already translated into different categories by the New Testament writers. The term has a long and revered pedigree, stemming from the earliest stages of Israel's history. God was King because of his decisive intervention in the history of his chosen people and their human experience.

Perhaps it would be more appropriate to speak of Yahweh's "reign" or "sovereignty" over his people. Unlike neighboring sovereigns who ruled by force of arms, subjugation and oppression, Yahweh's reign was based upon total annihilation of sin and evil, and on the unshakable presence of peace and justice. His Kingdom was not political or geographical; it was based on election. Israel was not a cowering, fearful people, terrified of its sovereign, but a "chosen people." "You shall be my special possession, dearer to me than all the other people, though all the earth is mine. You shall be to me a kingdom of priests, a holy nation" (Ex 19:5-6). The covenant established between God and Israel sealed a unique relationship between a loving sovereign and an obedient people, a union based on fidelity, not fear, on loving service, not slavery. While Israel had an important role to play in the continuation of this unique relationship, ultimately it depended on the transcending action of God. He was the sovereign Lord of the Kingdom.

But Israel's response was not that of a loving subject, a faithful covenant partner. Sin had destroyed that quality of harmony and integrity in its human experience known as "shalom" or peace which had always resulted from its genuine response to the covenant relationship. With the passage of centuries, Israel's prophets looked back with nostalgia for that "honeymoon period" between Yahweh and Israel. More so, based on God's fidelity to his promises, they looked ahead to a future epoch when people would truly live in harmony with God, with neighbor, with themselves and with the world. This new age would be characterized by peace and justice, by the obedient response of a righteous people, by the return of a paradisiacal epoch surpassing former periods in every way imaginable.

Israel's expectation based on the revelation of a great and glorious destiny was depicted in a variety of forms and images, too many to recount. In the words of Isaiah the prophet, a new Messianic age would be ruled by one named "Wonder-Counsellor, God-Hero, Father-Forever, Prince of Peace. His dominion [would be] vast and forever peaceful" (Is 9:5-6). "The Spirit of the Lord" would rest upon this Messianic ruler (Is 11:2), and he would initiate a Kingdom of utter bliss and harmony (Is 6:9). A variety of wonderful events characterizing restoration and harmony would be the hallmark of this new age:

> Then will the eyes of the blind be opened,
> the ears of the deaf be cleared;
> Then will the lame leap like a stag,
> then the tongue of the dumb will sing.
> (Is 35:5-6)
>
> The lowly will ever find joy in the LORD,
> and the poor rejoice in the Holy One of Israel.
> (Is 29:19)

Other prophets, like the celebrated Second Isaiah of the 6th century B.C., heralded the future age with poetic outpourings of a new creation and a new exodus (Is 40 - 55). The key theme was newness and rebirth. "See, the earlier things have come to pass, new ones I now foretell; before they spring into being, I announce them to you" (Is 42:9). Still others continued to revive hopes for the restoration of Israel as a holy people, a priestly people, with God alone as their ruler.

Toward the end of the Old Testament epoch, however, the concept of the kingly rule of Yahweh began to change. It was certain that God would decisively intervene in history. Yet no one really knew the time or the manner, and the resultant picture blurred. For some, God would appear in power and glory on a special day, the "Day of the Lord," a day of judgment and woe for sinners and Israel's enemies; a day of salvation and hope for the righteous servants of the Lord. For others, he would come only after this evil age was destroyed, and all of God's enemies were annihilated.

This new age would be accompanied by cosmic upheavals, strange signs and portents, catastrophes that defy description. The climactic moment of God's intervention was depicted in a new *genre* or style of writing called "apocalyptic," full of bizarre images: charged, violent and mysterious. Yahweh, the great warrior, would bring the Gentiles to their knees, and have them pay homage to the new theocratic Kingdom of Israel.

Just prior to the Christian era, Jewish literature heightened the tension and excitement by introducing secular and material notions to this Kingdom yet to come: Israel would be restored as a nation of power and glory. Thus, as the New Testament period approached, the atmosphere was charged with the hope and expectancy of a new age.

JESUS AND THE KINGDOM

When Jesus appeared on the scene, there was already a strong sense of the coming Kingdom. The prayer of every pious Jew was for Yahweh's speedy return. Anticipation of a Messiah was so keen at the time of Passover that additional Roman legionnaires were sent to Jerusalem for the feast to forestall any chance of rioting. By this time, the messianic concept had assumed strong political and nationalistic overtones. Patriotic and religious feelings meshed together. For some, God's reign meant freedom from the shackles of Rome; for others, it meant the restoration of Israel to a worldly power of times gone by. For others still, it meant revolution.

For Jesus, it was none of these; the Kingdom preached by Jesus was very different. Though outwardly proclaimed, its realm was within. Not temporal or spatial, not based on conquest or force of arms, it was founded on a new relationship between God and each human being. The Good News Jesus proclaimed about the Kingdom of God was predicated upon the sovereign will of God in one's life, making salvation available to all. "Shalom" or peace, that quality of relationship between God and the individual, resulting in harmony, integrity, wholeness, freedom from fear, anxiety and fragmentation, was made possible in the person of Jesus.

Sharing in the new Kingdom would call for an inner conversion, a radical change of lifestyle, a transformation of mind and heart, a reversal of selfish values. It would determine the way individuals would regard each other, their quality of concern, compassion and forgiveness of one another. It would ask them to leave everything behind and adopt its principles; it would provide its members with a joyful stance toward the future, no matter what.

Many heard the good news of the Kingdom, yet could not accept it. How could they, when it so countered their earthly and political expectations? What kind of a kingdom was this, based on humble service and love of neighbor? What kind of a king was this who spoke in parables, preached forgiveness and — to dramatize his convictions — even ate with publicans, prostitutes and sinners? We can understand why so many of Jesus' listeners were dismayed, why others misunderstood, and still others hated him. This "good news" was not at all what they had anticipated; it did not measure up to their personal expectations.

The Nature of the Kingdom

As mentioned previously, Jesus began his public ministry with the proclamation of the imminence of God's Kingdom. The frequency of this expression in the Synoptic Gospels underlies its major importance. After a brief prologue, Mark's Gospel opens with a summary of the Good News:

> The proper time has been fulfilled and the Kingdom of God has come; repent and believe in the good news! (1:15).

A similar announcement is attributed to Jesus in the accounts of Matthew and Luke:

> Repent, for the Kingdom of Heaven has come (Mt 4:17).

> I must give the good news of the Kingdom of God to the other cities, too, because I was sent for them (Lk 4:43).

All throughout the first three Gospels, the same expression occurs in a variety of different sayings and contexts: the Kingdom is near, but also far away; it is in your midst, yet you must pray for its coming; one must become like a child to enter it, yet the violent take it by force; to some the mystery of the Kingdom has been confided, yet no one knows the day or the hour of its coming. The concept's richness is illustrated repeatedly with new images. The Kingdom is likened to the arrival of harvest time, the blossoming of a fig tree, new wine, a new cloth, the best robe given to a son who had been lost but now was found, etc. The profusion and variety of expressions illustrating the Kingdom of God causes confusion. At the risk of oversimplification, we shall try to describe some of its characteristics.

Given by God

Jesus proclaimed a Kingdom given by God. Its coming into time, history and human experience is initiated by God. No one is born worthy of it; no one can earn or merit it; it is God's gift to humankind. G.K. Chesterton's adage, applied to the election of Israel in the Old Testament, might well be said of the Jews in Jesus' time. "How odd of God to choose the Jews." The Kingdom is in our midst because God is gracious! No matter how well motivated, one cannot create or build the Kingdom without the divine *fiat*. Throughout the ages people have tried in one form or another to establish a Christian Utopia, a kingdom on earth, modelled on that of God's Kingdom; but every attempt has been doomed to failure, as it was ultimately not God's plan. Like a little child, helpless and dependent, one receives this gift from a gracious God.

The Kingdom Is Present

A striking feature of Jesus' teaching about the Kingdom is its proximity. According to Mark, Jesus announced that the Kingdom "has come." In Luke's Gospel, when asked of the Kingdom's time, Jesus replied, "The Kingdom of God is in your midst." He spoke with dramatic certainty about God's Kingdom already present in the here and now. When the disciples of John the Baptist asked him, "Are you He who is to come, or are we to expect another?" Jesus replied to them, "Go tell John what you hear and see:

> **The blind can see again** and the lame walk,
> Lepers are made clean and the deaf hear,
> The dead are raised and **the poor are given
> the good news;**
> And blessed be whoever is not scandalized by me.
> (Mt 11:4-6; Lk 7:22-23)

Now was the time of salvation. In Jewish thinking the blind, the lame and the lepers were considered dead. Now help is extended to those in the depths of despair; now those who were as good as dead are raised to life. Even today, the consummation of the world is dawning. Not some distant far away reality, God's reign is available now for the asking.

To those who heard Jesus reading from the prophet Isaiah in the synagogue at Nazareth, the time of God's grace was fulfilled

today (Lk 4:21). The harvest had come; the fig tree puts forth
shoots; the new wine is offered; the wedding garment is put on
because the bridegroom is present. The peace of God is offered and
judgment is decreed because the true and genuine "shalom," long
sought by David and Solomon, by the many prophets and wise
men, has now become reality. It is as available to us today as it was
when Jesus first proclaimed it.

The Kingdom Is Yet To Come

While the present reality of the Kingdom is apparent, there
are other passages which suggest that it is also of the future. In the
very prayer given by Jesus to his disciples, we pray, "May your
Kingdom come" (Lk 11:2; Mt 6:10). He also said to them: "Amen,
I say to you, there are some who are standing here who will not
taste death until they see the Kingdom of God has come with
power" (Mk 9:1). In another place Jesus talks about Abraham,
Isaac and the prophets, along with the Gentiles, streaming in from
every direction to recline at table in the Kingdom of God (cf. Lk
13:28-29).

Jesus frequently spoke about the need to belong to the
Kingdom at the end of time (Mt 5:20; 7:21; 18:3; 19:23; 22:12),
and about the danger of being thrown into outer darkness (Mt
13:42; 22:13; 25:30). There are also passages where Jesus refers
to himself as the Son of Man who will appear as judge at the end
of time (Lk 12:8-9; Mt 10:32-33; also, Mk 14:62). (The *Son of
Man* expression was taken originally from the book of Daniel 7:13,
where it denotes a heavenly being who brings salvation and who
embodies in himself the Kingdom of the Saints of the Most High.)
This second coming would entail a general judgment of all people
and bring to a close the Kingdom as it exists on earth.

The "Already" and the "Not Yet"

Which opinion is correct? Is the Kingdom a present reality?
Is it yet to come at some future time? Or, are they both correct?
For as long as biblical scholars have discussed the subject, there

have been proponents for either side. The pendulum has swung to both extremes. The truth lies somewhere in the middle.

There are those who insist that Jesus regarded the Kingdom as wholly present, and the "futurist" sayings were simply later additions of the early Church. There are also those who see the Kingdom as an entirely future reality, an event which lies outside history and closes it. Jesus, in the latter opinion, would then have been an apocalyptic preacher, proclaiming a single, shattering action of God, which would create his Kingdom at the same time as it ended all world history. According to this opinion, Jesus' disciples would have modified and altered his statements after the crucifixion, when the end of the ages did not come.

Without going into a detailed analysis of the texts, the truth of the matter is that Jesus saw a present and a future side of the Kingdom. God's reign is being actualized in the lives of men and women now, but there is more to come. It is in the process of becoming; its full realization remains ahead, at what time or manner no one knows. The important point is that it is already in our midst. Once, on being asked by the Pharisees when the reign of God would come, Jesus replied: "The Kingdom of God is not coming in a way that can be observed, nor will they say, 'Look, here it is!' or, 'There it is!' — behold, the Kingdom of God is in your midst!" (Lk 17:20-21).

In the words and works of Jesus, people were already beginning to realize what God's Kingdom meant, the tremendous possibilities it offered for the future. Such was what made his words and deeds so significant. Through him God was already speaking and working. Now was the time to respond.

In fact, because the Kingdom is already present, and yet not fully realized, there will always be a tension in the human experience of a person who acknowledges the reality and demands of the Kingdom. The tension is between the "already" and the "not yet," between a promise believed and lived and a fullness still to come, between hope for future glory and the disillusionment over present failures. There is a struggle involved to make of the Kingdom all that it should be, but unfortunately is not. The work is divinely initiated. It cannot fail because of frail human response: sin, selfishness and countless other deficiencies. The struggle continues. Such is the point of the parable of the sower; it all depends where the seed falls. The growth of the Kingdom does not always go well, at least by our standards, but it continues. It must continue, in spite of human obstacles, because it is divinely initiated.

Human Response: Conversion

The second part of Jesus' public proclamation about the Kingdom of God concerns our human response: "Reform your lives and believe in the good news." The theme of repentance (inner reform, conversion) is our fundamental response to the Kingdom. The Greek word which was used, *metanoia*, implies a complete change of life, a turning from sin and a surrender to God's will. Without *metanoia*, true discipleship is impossible; without a radical inner renewal, it is hardly likely that one will ever come to "know Jesus Christ."

All too often, we try to make the life history or biography of Jesus the object of our study without reference to his message. Jesus' message is that we must "reform our lives." He makes us ask questions about ourselves before revealing himself as the answer to those questions. Is it any wonder that the concept of the Kingdom of God plays such a central role in the teaching of Jesus? The quality of our response will determine the quality of our Christian discipleship.

The terms "repentance" or "conversion" have been used so frequently in popular jargon that it has become watered down. What is entailed is a *total* change of mind and heart. One does not merely repent of one's sins, but of what one is. The change is radical; it calls for a fundamental reversal of life's values; it demands a personal revolution. Only in this sense can Jesus be called a revolutionary, because he called for a substantial change in our inner life, a change which will and must have external consequences: in our values, our attitudes, our outlook and the way we regard other people.

When I say "yes" to the invitation extended by Jesus in his Kingdom message, I enter into a vitally new, personal relationship with God. By my acceptance of Jesus and his message, I place my total trust and confidence in God as my gracious and personal Father. He becomes the ground of my being, the basis for my identity as a believer. As incredible as it sounds, the Father of Jesus becomes our Father, our *Abba* (an Aramaic diminutive for father, loosely translated as "Daddy"). I can speak to him openly and honestly. Fear and anxiety, the disastrous consequences of sin, are transformed. Evil still remains; at times it may even seem to have the upper hand. Present circumstances may still appear chaotic and unpredictable; the future still remains uncertain and mysterious. But, because of the extraordinary manifestation of God as gracious and benign, my fears are transformed; my basic life response in face of pain, suffering and death, is one of hope; my stance toward the future is drastically altered; it is permeated with a serene and confident joy. No matter what happens, God's sovereign will shall prevail. He has assured me in the good news of his Son, Jesus Christ, that this is so. And in that promise I believe.

There is a radical newness to my life. I now think differently and act differently. I view the world and people differently. My attitudes and values change in conformity with the tenets of the Kingdom. I view my own identity and personhood differently. I am loved by a gracious God! My life is destined for "shalom": peace, integrity, wholeness. Realism has not disappeared. My outlook on the world has not become simplistic, naïve or rosycolored. My struggles with sin and selfishness still remain. However, the revelation of God in Jesus has permeated my inner being with grace. For a believer, the recognition and personal acceptance of the reality of God's Kingdom as already present makes all the difference in the world.

The Kingdom and the Spirit

As we have already seen in the first three chapters on Gospel formation, the message of Jesus was already being recast and reformulated soon after the resurrection. Such a process was inevitable if the message was to continue in time. The post-Easter community grew and developed in its awareness of the significance of Jesus and his message to a degree that was not quite possible during his earthly ministry.

The Jesus who *preached* was now the Jesus who *was preached*! The Jesus of history, who called for radical inner conversion and total submission to the will of the Father, was now the Christ of faith: the way, the truth and the life of the Father. Whereas Jesus preached the nearness of God's Kingdom, the early Church preferred to offer men and women the personal experience of the Spirit. Jesus, the proclaimer of the Kingdom, by his death, resurrection, ascension and sending of the Holy Spirit made possible a vitally new relationship between God and humankind.

In such a brief discussion of the Gospel concept of the Kingdom of God, one can hardly do justice to the gradual metamorphosis from the reign of God to the reign of the Spirit. The close relation existing between the Spirit and the Kingdom calls for a more deliberate analysis of Paul's letters, the Gospel of John and the other New Testament works. However brief, a sampling of Paul's thought will serve our purposes here.

For Paul, the Spirit prepares a person for the Kingdom: to inherit the Kingdom in the future, an individual must experience the work of the Spirit in the present (1 Cor 6:9-11). And that work of the Spirit, first begun at conversion and initiation, must continue throughout the Christian's life (Gal 5:16-23). That is why Paul can describe the Kingdom in terms of the Christian's present experience of the Spirit: "The Kingdom of God is not eating and drinking, but justice, peace and joy in the Holy Spirit" (Rm 14:17).

The Spirit, we might say, is the "present-ness" of the Kingdom. Where the Spirit is, the Kingdom is, so that to have the Spirit is to have part and lot in the Kingdom here and now. The presence of the Spirit is the "already" of the Kingdom; the inadequacy of our recognition of the Spirit's presence and submission to that Spirit explains the "not yet" of the Kingdom. The Kingdom is present to us in Jesus through his Spirit. Where the Spirit of Jesus is, there is the Kingdom.

In other words, by sharing the life of the Holy Spirit, the Spirit of Jesus, we are allowed to share in the very life of God as far as this is humanly possible. As mentioned before, God, in a very special sense, becomes our Father. Such is our privilege because we share the life of his Son now made available through the Spirit. In a certain sense, Jesus Christ becomes our adopted brother through the gift of life we share. And all of those who also enjoy this life become our brothers and sisters in Christ. Through the gift of the Kingdom proclaimed and now made available in and through the Spirit of Jesus, we become as one family of God. And here lies the basis for true Christian community as well as the dynamism for that quality of relationship which should exist between the members of such a community.

What seemed like a quaint expression of a bygone age, the Kingdom of God, becomes eminently personal. As happens so frequently, biblical terminology has to be dislodged from its historical, literary and cultural context and translated into twentieth century categories. If the expression reflects a valid experience of people who were confronted with an explosive message which shook the core of their beings, there is no reason why that experience cannot be made our own. If the reign of God suggests a vitally new relationship with God and others, with oneself and with the world, if it suggests attainment of "shalom," in the fullest sense of that rich biblical word, what could be more important? Is there anything more meaningful in life than the way we live with God and with one another? Only the quality of our relationship with God and with one another will determine the degree to which we share in the life of God here on earth, to say nothing of the hereafter.

The Kingdom and the Church

Before concluding our discussion of the Kingdom of God, there is still a final question to be considered. What is the relationship between the Kingdom and the Church? The question is of major importance because it touches on the mission of the Church today.

Is the reign of God identical with the Church? A certain critic of the Church at the turn of this century wrote that Jesus proclaimed the Kingdom, but what came out was the Catholic

Church. The New Testament, however, never identifies the reign of God and the Church. The reign of God is larger than the Church; the Church is subject to the reign, and is not the final realization of the reign of God.

Although not perfectly identical, neither are they perfectly distinct. The Church has a close relationship to the reign of God. Jesus came to proclaim the good news of the reign, and the effect of his work was to establish a community of believers, a Church, to continue his mission for future ages. The primary function and role of the Church is to continue the proclamation of the reign which Jesus initiated, and to carry on his teaching. The role of the Church is to foster and promote the reality of the reign in every way possible and through every means at its disposal. In the "Pastoral Constitution on the Church in the Modern World," promulgated by the Second Vatican Council, we read: "... the Church has a single intention: That God's Kingdom may come to pass, and that the salvation of the whole human race may come to pass" (*Gaudium et Spes*, art. 45, par. 1).

Unfortunately, through human neglect, the Church's mission has sometimes become hazy and undefined, its radical Gospel objectives sometimes neglected. There have been times when the Church was unduly preoccupied with conversions and the swelling of its own ranks, when quantitative membership seemed more important than qualitative relationship to the person of Jesus Christ. There have been times when the Church has been too concerned about promoting its own ends, its own aggrandizement, its own establishment. But the Church does not exist for its own sake. It is a servant of the Kingdom, and was established for the sake of the Kingdom. All of its resources, personnel and structures are intended for promoting the reality of the Kingdom of God here on earth. When it begins forgetting the notion of the reign of God, then its mission becomes unclear, and its members become confused and uncertain about their own identities and roles.

Perhaps a return to the very fundamental message of Jesus as seen in the Gospels will help us better to understand our duties and responsibilities as members of the Church. No matter who we are, what ministry we enjoy in the Church, as long as we profess belief in Jesus Christ, we are called to be disciples of the Kingdom, and to bear witness to it in accord with our position in life. The way we respond to the Kingdom message is very much related to the way we experience Jesus Christ today.

QUESTIONS FOR DISCUSSION

1. How do you understand the notion of the "Kingdom of God"? What significance does it have in terms of your own human experience?

2. Why did Jesus use so many different images to describe the Kingdom? In your opinion, what is the most effective way of communicating the Kingdom concept in our own times?

3. Do you see the reign of God as "already in your midst"? In what way?

4. How do you understand the tension between the "already" and the "not yet" of the Kingdom in your own personal experience?

5. Can you speak of the biblical notion of "conversion" from personal experience?

6. How can the Church best promote the concept of the reign of God in our own times? Has it done so successfully?

7. How do you understand your own role as sharing in the mission of the Church?

Chapter V

PARABLES:
WORDS OF THE KINGDOM

Mark 4;   Matthew 13; 20:1-16;   Luke 11:33-36; 12 - 20

*I*n the previous chapter we considered the central aspect of the teaching of Jesus concerning the Kingdom of God. Of the many descriptive titles applied to Jesus through the centuries, the one that sums up his historical appearance best is: Jesus as the Proclaimer of the Kingdom of God. The good news was that God had intervened once again in time, history and human experience in the person of Jesus Christ, and through him established a vitally new relationship between God and ourselves. Not only was such a reality coming; it was already present.

But what was the nature of this new relationship? How did the people of Jesus' time experience it? How did they react to it? What kind of a personal response would be entailed? And how did Jesus communicate the message of the reign to the men and women of his age?

A correct understanding and interpretation of the parables will answer some of these questions because they are concerned primarily with the Kingdom. Not only the parables, but also the miracles as well as the moral teaching of Jesus have as their central point the reality of the Kingdom as we shall see in the next two chapters.

What are parables? Why did Jesus use them so frequently? For Jesus' disciples the parables were by their nature well-

designed to convey the challenging, confronting, decision-provoking reality of the Kingdom of God. In their own inimitable way
they imparted to their hearers something of Jesus' vision of the
power of God, experienced by those who were confronted by the
reality of this proclamation. They tell us how people reacted when
faced with that message. They illustrate in a variety of metaphors
and symbols the many-faceted quality of response called for from
disciples who have said "yes" to the Kingdom invitation.

Our consideration of parables should give us a better understanding of Jesus Christ, but not as a historical figure of the past,
a story book personality, a portrait of a first century Palestinian
prophet/teacher touched up by biblical scholars. Parables illustrate the dynamic of a person and his message by other believing
persons. If the Gospels are truly the recorded expression of the
faith and experience of those who confronted Jesus, we too must
try to integrate that experience and make it our own, if we are to
be his true disciples. There is no other way to encounter the Jesus
of the Gospels. The parables contain a certain explosive quality
because they have captured in a unique way some of the vital
power of God's reign. Our discussion will try to ignite some of that
power and transform it into our own personal experience.

WHAT IS A PARABLE?

One of the favorite techniques used by Jesus to communicate
the message of God's reign was the parable. Altogether some fifty
to seventy parables appear in the Gospels, depending on the
manner of classification. The word "parable" takes its meaning
from a Hebrew expression (*mashal*) which includes a wide variety
of figures of speech: similes (Mt 13:33), metaphors (Mt 5:14),
proverbs (Lk 4:23), maxims (Lk 14:7-11), examples (Lk 12:15-
21), and riddles (Mk 7:15-17). Many of these are not strictly
parables and so, when they are included, the number of "parables"
is enlarged.

In the traditional teaching of the Church for centuries,
parables were treated as allegories in which each character and
detail had an assigned meaning. A decoding process was neces-

sary. But allegorization was not something original with the parables. It set in when parables were taken out of their early Semitic setting and placed into a non-Jewish environment.

The parable was originally simple, having one point of comparison, a developed simile where the story, while fictitious, is true to life (e.g., the Kingdom of God is like a mustard seed, or like a pearl of great price, or like the sower who went out to sow seed). The parable tells a story which turns upon a point which has its parallel or analogy within the experience of those to whom it is addressed. The message of the parable becomes clear once this central turning point is grasped. Allegory tends to be complex and needs a key to be decoded. In the parable the characters and details have no figurative meaning; the important thing is the lesson of the story. The rule is not hard and fast because, in some few instances, allegorizing tendencies began to set into the parables of Jesus from the beginning; but, for the most part, the parallel or analogy was not explained. The normal practice of Jesus was to end the parable inconclusively, allowing the hearers to grasp the point and to find the analogy for themselves.

PARABLES OF JESUS

In their original setting and for their audiences, parables were simple, colorful illustrations of Jesus' teaching. They had a certain freshness, candor, down-to-earth quality and simplicity that twenty-first century Westerners cannot always appreciate. Not merely because we are so removed in time and culture from first century Palestine, but also because we tend to be more analytic, discursive and scientific in our thinking. Where the Western mind formulates a definition, a syllogism, an equation, the Oriental draws a picture, using a riddle or an illustration to convey the point. They were early practitioners of the adage: "One picture is worth a thousand words."

Parables are made up of illustrations taken from the daily life of first century Palestine: leaven, fishing nets, lamps, pearls, lilies of the field, mustard seeds, children in the marketplace, Samaritans, publicans, laborers and merchants. They attract a hearer's attention by their vividness and graphic quality. They offer an analogy or a point of comparison, but they do not give the answer. They tantalize; they arouse curiosity; there is usually an unexpected twist which leaves the hearer in sufficient doubt about the precise application; they tease the mind into thought. The listener has to concede a point which, on first hearing, does not seem applicable to his or her life. There is a slow fuse built into the parable. It burns slowly and smokes a little before igniting. It catches the listener by surprise and then traps him or her into thinking, reflecting and then eventually asking: "Now that couldn't apply to me... or could it?" Then the import of the message hits home: "Yes, it does apply to me, very much so!"

The parables were so adequate for proclaiming the notion of the Kingdom because they were so much in tune with the life and needs of the people encountered by Jesus. He spoke to them "just where they were at," no obfuscation, no pretentiousness, no religious jargon, no convoluted clerical language.

In the language of the parables, the Kingdom of God was likened to the processes of nature, or to the experiences of ordinary peasant life familiar to everyone. Jesus did not think it necessary to create artificial illustrations for the truths he wished to teach. There is in the parables a certain sacredness and reverence for the simple things of life. What better way to communicate the deeper reality of the Kingdom than to show how it develops and grows out of the ordinary aspects of life? Much can be learned by preachers and teachers about the importance of communicating religious values in the ordinary language and parlance of the people from Jesus' use of parables.

VARIATIONS IN PARABLES

Although the simple parable had only one point of comparison — unlike the allegory where every character or figure had a different meaning — the obvious point is not always apparent because of "transmission problems." We have already seen in the first three chapters on Gospel formation, the process of growth and development of the Jesus traditions from the time of the public

ministry to the time of their final written expression by the
evangelists, a span ranging from thirty-five to fifty-five years.
During this time-span the parables "lived" in different settings.
There could have been as many as three: the original setting in the
ministry of Jesus, a later setting given the parables by the apostolic
preachers and teachers, and then the final audience addressed by
the evangelist.

The words of Jesus, as we have seen already, were not static;
they were dynamic, challenging and alive. They were filtered
through the prism of a growing and changing community. And, in
their passage, they were continually transformed and modified.
Quite understandably so. While the substance of Jesus' message
was the same, different audiences with different needs necessitated slight variations and modifications in one and the same
parable. While it may not be possible today to set apart these
different settings clearly, there is sufficient evidence to indicate
their presence. Knowing this helps us to understand the frequent
variations in the parables.

For example, many of the parables preached by Jesus were
undoubtedly aimed at the Pharisees and their refusal to accept the
reality of the Kingdom. These same parables were re-used by
Church leaders in the fifties and sixties and directed to the
Christian community at large, when the importance of the Pharisees had waned. For example, in Luke 15:3-7 the "lost sheep"
refers to outcasts and sinners rejected by the Pharisees. But in
Matthew (18:12-14) the phrase "lost sheep" refers to errant
Christians who must be given special attention by Church authorities. The central concern for those considered "lost" is the
same, though the term "lost sheep" refers to a different group in
Matthew because of the new setting and problems of his audience.

Other modifications were introduced because of a new
language (the change from Aramaic to Greek), new cultural
settings (Jewish Palestinian to Hellenistic Gentile), new audiences
(Matthew's Jewish converts and Luke's Gentiles). As a result, the
same parable may have different meanings in different Gospels;
e.g., compare the parable of the lamp in Mk 4:21 with Mt 5:10-
16 and Lk 11:23. In such cases it is difficult to decide which was
the original setting of the parable in the life of Jesus. No matter.

Biblical truth does not depend on historical accuracy alone, but on the faithful interpretation of the mind of Jesus and the application of that mind to differing Christian needs.

In some cases, an original sense of immediacy and call to repentance associated with the sudden and imminent coming of the Lord's reign has been changed to an exhortation and encouragement, preparing the later Christian community for the long haul. It was becoming apparent that the final coming of the Lord might not come soon.

Such is the key to the interpretation of the somewhat difficult parable of the Unjust Steward (Lk 16:1-8). Originally it ended with Luke 16:8a: "And the lord commended the dishonest steward because he'd acted wisely!" In other words, this is the resolute way you should act when confronted with the reality of the Kingdom! The cryptic ending of the original parable of Jesus invited other additions to bring out the meaning more precisely. For example, Luke 16:8b contains the wish that Christians (not the original audience of Jesus' parable) act as wisely and boldly in their lives as do "the children of this world." The next comment (Lk 16:9) is an exhortation to use material means wisely and generously, as is befitting disciples of the Lord. Then the third application (Lk 16:10-12) deals with the general theme of faithfulness in all that is entrusted to one in life. And the final application (Lk 16:13), also found in Matthew's account of the Sermon on the Mount (6:24), tells how one must decide between God or mammon!

No wonder modern hearers are so frequently confused by this parable! All of these later applications probably originated with Jesus, but they were not a part of the original parable. An unusual example, indeed, but one which bears out the fluidity and flexibility of the living words of Jesus, and their application by the Gospel writers.

The same thing applies to such floating maxims as, "Everyone who exalts himself shall be humbled" found in different settings (in Lk 18:14 and 14:11; and in Mt 23:12); or, "The last will be first and the first last" (Mt 19:30; Mk 10:31; Lk 13:30); and finally, "Many are called but few are chosen" (Mt 22:14 and 20:16b). Hardly a dead letter, the words of Jesus were alive, full of meaning, and thereby applicable to many new situations far removed from their original context.

THE RESPONSE ASKED FOR IN THE PARABLES

Like a precious diamond which shimmers and sparkles when placed in sunlight, casting its colors and shades in many different directions, so too, the reality of the Kingdom of God communicated in parables is multi-faceted. Even isolating some of the key aspects and placing them into a logical order for pedagogical purposes is doing somewhat of an injustice to the full reality. Admitting the problem, let us try nonetheless to single out some of the essential aspects of the Kingdom, as well as the qualitative response it evokes in the experience of its hearers.

How did the parables touch the lives of Jesus' disciples? What were men and women of the Kingdom like? Can we make their response a viable experience for our own times? If the reality of the Kingdom established a vitally new relationship between God and ourselves, our understanding of the parables should present us with a certain new outlook, a vision, a set of attitudes, a value system, an orientation to God, to ourselves and to one another. It may help us understand the significance of Jesus Christ in our lives today.

Joy
> The Parable of the Hidden Treasure and
> the Parable of the Pearl (Mt 13:44-46).

Both of these parables illustrate the genuine surprise and joy that come from the recognition of God's Kingdom as a present reality. Unexpectedly, without any advance notice, one comes upon a treasure. What a stroke of good fortune! It's like a hidden dream come true. The immediate response is to drop everything and to invest oneself totally in this new found possession. Such is the reaction of the disciple who discovers the reality of God's reign and who embraces it with joyful abandonment, for he has found a treasure more precious than anything else in the world.

One wonders why it is that so few believers reflect the joyful discovery of God's reign in their lifestyle. Is it really such a precious possession to them? Does it make any difference at all? After all, he *has* come, hasn't he? Then why are there so many harbingers of doom, cynics, pessimists among those who call themselves his followers? Why are we so anxious, gloomy, full of trepidation, fearful about the future? If we have found him, why not share him with joy-filled hearts? Perhaps there is something to the saying one hears today: "It's not God who's dead; his people are!"

Attitudes of Forgiveness

> The Parable of the Lost Sheep (Lk 15:3-7; Mt 18:12-14),
> The Lost Coin (Lk 15:8-10),
> The Prodigal Son (Lk 15:11-32),
> The Two Debtors (Lk 7:41-43),
> The Unmerciful Servant (Mt 18:23-35).

One of the clearest signs of the reality of the Kingdom is the manifestation of God as a forgiving Father. If one were to ask, "How is the kingly activity of God primarily known?" Jesus would answer, "In the forgiveness of sins." It was good news, indeed, when Jesus revealed the reconciling will of his Father, calling sinners to himself, assuring mercy and forgiveness beyond measure, willing to forgive not just seven times, but seventy times seven times... without limit.

Men and women are challenged to a new relationship with God and with one another, made possible by the present reality of God's forgiveness. God doesn't force it on anyone; it must be freely accepted, and it presupposes a total change of mind and heart. Those who have received the forgiveness of the Kingdom are to share it; there is no room for standing on personal rights or prerogatives.

As a background for the proper interpretation of these parables, it might be well to remember that for the religious authorities of Jesus' time, there were certain reprehensible types for whom God's forgiveness was impossible. No amount of prayer, almsgiving, expiatory rites or other forms of repentance could pardon certain odious characters, generally labelled as "tax-collectors and other Jews who had made themselves Gentiles." (The list might also include harlots, extortioners, swindlers, murders.) Indictment of tax-collectors was especially harsh because they were considered traitors. They had prostituted themselves and defiled their Jewish heritage by extorting money from their own countrymen to fill the coffers of the hated Romans. But all were simply branded "sinners," and any type of association with the likes of these would defile a person.

What was absolutely shocking to the scribes and Pharisees was that Jesus not only welcomed such outcasts of society, but he actually invited them to break bread with him, thereby shattering the religious standards of his contemporaries. One must remember that, for pious Jews, eating at the same table with such "sinners" was tantamount to blasphemy.

The parables listed above are most often directed against the scribes and Pharisees, who considered Jesus' attitude totally unacceptable. The context is generally one of conflict. They are extreme examples of the challenge of the forgiveness of sins offered in the proclamation of Jesus. Scribe, tax-collector, harlot, zealot and fisherman came and sat at the same table, at which they celebrated the joy of the present experience of forgiveness and anticipated its consummation in the future.

When we see such examples of forgiveness as Jesus had shown, we recognize one of the basic signs of the present reality of God's Kingdom. We pray daily: "Forgive us our trespasses, as we are also willing to forgive those who hurt us." But do we? How far are we willing to forgive? Seventy times seven, without limit? How do we regard the "sinners" of our own day? Those who don't conform to our preconceived standards? Does the Church foster and promote the reality of the Kingdom by the quality of forgiveness shown by its members?

In the following parables we shall consider certain aspects of the reign of God, where the emphasis is more directly upon the experience of the hearer — his or her reaction to the challenge of the Kingdom.

WHAT ARE MEN AND WOMEN OF THE KINGDOM LIKE?

They show resolute action while there is still time.

> The Parable of the Great Supper (Mt 22:1-14;
> Lk 14:16-24),
> The Ten Virgins (Mt 15:1-12),
> The Unjust Steward (Lk 16:1-9),
> The Rich Man and Lazarus (Lk 16:19-31).

The gracious invitation extended by the Father to share in the reality of the Kingdom calls for an immediate decision. There is an urgency to the present situation; there can be no dilly-dallying. Once the joyful reality of God's reign is recognized, there is no holding back. One must make a decision for or against. *Now!* What would be the effect on society if all the so-called "committed Christians" responded freely, joyfully and totally to the challenge of the Kingdom?

They are ready to respond to the challenge of discipleship.

> The Parable of the Good Samaritan (Lk 10:25-37),
> The Unmerciful Servant (Mt 18:23-35),
> The Tower Builder (Lk 14:28-32).

These parables emphasize certain qualities of active discipleship: an earnestness, self-preparedness, sensitivity to need and the willingness to respond with alacrity; a joyous, serving, active faith; love and concern unlimited, without any notion of self-righteousness or rules to be fulfilled.

The sole criterion is need. To the question of "Who is my neighbor?", which introduces the parable of the Good Samaritan, Jesus does not answer with some theoretical construct of neighborliness. He shifts the answer around in the form of an illustration: Who proved to be the neighbor? Those who enjoy the gracious touch of God's action in the person of Jesus must respond, not by asking questions about the limits of love and responsibility, not by waiting for rules or regulations, not by looking for the "Church" to respond, but by asking themselves: "Who has need of me?" In other words, I must put myself in the place of the suffering, the helpless, the needy, and then get to work.

Is it realistic for Christians to respond in this way? How many have really tried?

They have total trust in the reality of God's presence.

> The Parable of the Unjust Judge (Lk 18:1-8),
> The Friend at Midnight (Lk 11:5-8).

This quality of discipleship is intimately tied up with trust in God: to believe that God is, indeed, active in the ministry of Jesus, and that Jesus has actuated a vitally new relationship between God and humankind.

Faith in these parables does not suggest an acknowledgment of God or Jesus as some abstract reality, as some faraway being, but as a reality in the here-and-now, a belief that is founded in the continued presence of the Spirit of Jesus in the situations, events and human encounters of daily life. Such a belief leads to an obedient response, manifesting itself in a variety of attitudes and outlooks indicative of the present reality of the Kingdom. Such is the quality of the following sayings, which are not strictly parables, but which, nonetheless, illustrate graphically the various aspects of genuine discipleship.

a. No one who puts his hand to the plow and looks behind is fit for the Kingdom of God (Lk 9:62).

This saying characterizes the single-mindedness and determination that is an essential aspect of the response to the challenge.

b. It's easier for a camel to go through a needle's eye than it is for a rich man to go into the Kingdom of God (Mk 10:23-25).

How many Christians have given serious consideration to this one? So typical of the image-making ability of the wise man of the East! We have no law or regulation, simply a warning: absolute self-surrender and the placing of one's total trust in the

Lord becomes much more difficult to one hindered and weighed down by riches.

  c. Let the dead bury their own dead, but *you*, go proclaim the Kingdom of God! (Lk 9:60).

To get the full point of this saying, one would have to appreciate the seriousness of Jewish laws about contact with dead bodies, as well as the binding obligation to bury one's close of kin. The response to the challenge is all demanding; it must transcend all other duties and responsibilities, however naturally and normally important they might be.

They show a radically new approach to the business of living.

  Included below are a few brief sayings, parabolic in the broadest sense of the term, illustrating certain distinctive attitudes proper to a disciple of the Kingdom.

  1. Amen, I say to you, whoever doesn't accept the Kingdom of God like a child shall not enter it! (Mk 10:15).

There is no suggestion here of returning to childhood. Hardly! But like a child that instinctively depends on parents, so too, the lifestyle of one who is living the "Kingdom way" is founded upon a complete obedience and total dependence on God as the end-all and be-all of everything.

  2. But I tell you *not* to resist the evildoer; on the contrary,

> Whoever strikes you on the right cheek,
>   turn the other to him as well;
> To the one who wants to go to law with you
> and take your tunic,
>   give him your cloak as well,
> And whoever forces you to go one mile,
>   go with him two....
> I say to you,
>   Love your enemies,
>   And pray for those who persecute you,

so that you'll become sons of your Father in Heaven,
because
He causes His sun to rise on the evil and the good,
    and rains on the just and the unjust.
For if you love those who love you,
what reward will you have?
    Don't the tax-collectors also do the same?
And if you greet only your brothers,
what great thing are you doing?
    Don't the Gentiles also do the same?
So *you* be perfect
    as your Heavenly Father is perfect.
                     (Mt 5:39-41, 44-48)

These sayings, among the most radical in the entire New Testament, touch on some of the most difficult aspects of response to the Kingdom experience. If asked how far one is expected to go, these sayings illustrate the limits: they are boundless. They are not meant to be rules, regulations, or commandments. Actually, rules would be much easier, because the limits are defined. But an illustration knows no limits; no boundaries are imposed. It simply conveys an attitude that is to be taken seriously.

These are radical demands of the Kingdom, proposing a radically new approach to the business of living. They offer no specifics or details about how one is to respond. Nor for that matter, do they issue sanctions for not complying. They simply illustrate the radically new life attitudes resulting from Jesus' challenges of the Kingdom. More will be said on this point when we consider the moral teaching of Jesus in Chapter Seven.

They stop depending on their own pre-conceived ideas.

    The Parable of the Laborers in the Vineyard
        (Mt 20:1-16),
    The Children in the Marketplace
        (Mt 11:16-19; Lk 7:31-35),
    The Pharisee and the Tax-Collector
        (Lk 18:9-14).

One of the basic attitudes of a genuine disciple is illustrated in the parable of the laborers in the vineyard. The unexpected twist in the story frequently leads to misunderstanding on the part of today's hearer. One might think there has been a violation of fair labor practices, because those who worked the entire day received the same wage as those who worked a mere hour. The issue at stake, however, is not about the laborers in the vineyard, or their salaries, but the goodness, graciousness and generosity of the employer. He has given something not bargained for, not even promised, beyond the wildest dreams. By human standards of justice, it might not make sense, but the largesse of God's love is not limited by such strictures.

So, then, drop your preconceived ideas and clearly held preconceptions about what is right and what is wrong, and follow the "Kingdom way." Stop being so smug and complacent, as if you had all the answers. Don't be deceived into thinking that your exact, though perfunctory, fulfillment of rules and obligations will make you pleasing before God. Accept the reality of the Kingdom, and act accordingly. But remember, you are to follow the Lord's standards and not your own. Unfortunately, there is always that proclivity in us to model ourselves on our own image and likeness, rather than God's.

They face an uncertain future with hope.

> The Parable of the Sower (Mk 4:3-20, 26-29),
> The Mustard Seed (Mk 4:30-32),
> The Leaven (Mt 13:33).

The so-called "Parables of Growth" are more properly termed "Parables of Contrast" because they offer the assurance that God's power will bring the Kingdom to pass, in spite of the seemingly insignificant beginnings in the ministry of Jesus. The real point is the contrast between the humble beginnings in the ministry of one who associated with the poor, the helpless and the outcasts of society, and the certain rich harvest which God will accomplish.

One might also include here those parables and sayings

which deal with the future realization of the Kingdom, e.g., Luke 13:28-29 and Matthew 8:11. As we saw in the previous chapter, there is tension between the "already" and the "not yet" of the Kingdom. The whole tenor of Jesus' teaching is that the experience of the present is an anticipation of the future. The disciple prays *now*, "May your Kingdom come." Table fellowship is a prelude, a foretaste of that ultimate heavenly banquet. The Kingdom is already here, and yet it has not been fully realized.

This emphasis on the future, however, is not one for which we can prepare. There are no blueprints for the future of the Kingdom; there is no warranty for smugness or self-deluding confidence about what lies ahead. We are not suggesting a naïve, simplistic outlook toward the future. The emphasis is on the present, which carries with it a guarantee for the future. The present that has become God's present guarantees that all futures will be God's futures. If such be the profound experience of people who have confronted the challenge of the Kingdom, then our stance toward the future, no matter how uncertain it may appear, must be one of genuine hope. In light of present circumstances, do we, as members of the Church whose mission it is to testify to the present reality of the Kingdom, give evidence of a hopeful attitude toward the future?

CONCLUDING COMMENTS

We have tried in this chapter to convey a variety of experiences which identify a disciple of the Kingdom. The power of God manifest in Jesus' proclamation of the Kingdom has graced the human person in such a way that the sum quality of one's response, the way he or she confronts God and signals the present reality of the Kingdom, is changed. In the midst of such a people, God's reign is apparent! They must be a people whose attitudes, outlook and approach to life is permeated with the urgency and necessity of the Kingdom. Their lifestyle must reveal an inner joy, a forgiving attitude without limits and exceptions, deep concern for the needs of others, a radical trust in God's presence in the normal day-to-day circumstances of life, a vision of hope for the future. Such a posture toward life could revolutionize society. In no other way can the followers of Jesus be called revolutionaries. However, imagine the practical consequences in society were such attitudes to be realized!

To know Jesus Christ is not so much a matter of reading his biography, gazing upon his portrait, or reconstructing, as far as possible, his history on the basis of critical biblical scholarship. We come to know Jesus Christ by sharing in the experience of those who were confronted by the urgency and import of his proclamation of the Kingdom. The same Spirit who guided those first hearers of the parables and enabled them to respond, continues to guide his disciples today. Through his Spirit, the Jesus who spoke in parables is present to us in his Word today. Incredible as it may seem, we can experience him just as vitally today as did his disciples after his departure from this earth.

QUESTIONS FOR DISCUSSION

1. Can you give examples of contemporary parables? Are they effective for communicating religious truths and values?

2. Can you give an example of a story or an illustration which changed because of a different "life setting"? How does it compare with the use of parables in different settings?

3. Is true inner joy reflective of the reality of God's reign among people? How about forgiveness? Can you give some examples?

4. What is the most effective way of communicating the reality of God's Kingdom in our society?

5. How is the reality of the Kingdom most evident in your own personal experience?

6. Can these qualities of discipleship communicated in parables be lived in our own times? Are they realistic?

7. How does one come to "know Jesus Christ" in the parables? Does this make the Scriptures a "living word"?

Chapter VI

MIRACLES: SIGNS OF THE KINGDOM

Mark 1:23; 2:12; 3:1-30; 5; 6; 8:1-30;
Matthew 8; 9; 14:13-36; 15:21-39;   Luke 11:14-26

*A*ccording to the Synoptic writers, the miracles performed by Jesus of Nazareth were signs of the present reality of God's Kingdom. Both parables and miracles are connected with the revelation of Jesus as the Proclaimer of the Kingdom, the Messiah of word and deed. In the previous chapter, we discussed that unique quality of relationship between God and humankind, and the subsequent experience of those disciples confronted by Jesus' parables. Now we will consider the miracles he performed. What are miracles? How were they understood in Jesus' time? How did they signal the presence of God's reign?

Severed from Jesus' general message and viewed in terms which ignore their first century Gospel setting, miracles have frequently been the basis for sharp attacks on Christianity. How could anyone perform healings and cures, raise people from the dead, walk on water and pacify raging storms, when these acts are obviously beyond the laws of nature? Either the description of miracle narratives represents a classic case of Semitic exaggeration, or the events themselves are instances of auto-suggestion, or unique situations, inexplicable to the primitive mind, but clearly demonstrable to modern science and medicine.

For some, miracles have been, quite frankly, a source of embarrassment, quickly passed over as "matters of faith," or ingeniously demythologized, i.e., explained away in terms of subjective personal experience. The traditional posture of Christianity, especially in this past century, was to consider miracles as apologetic proofs for the divinity of Jesus. Classic manuals of theology showed how miracles were beyond the laws of nature. Only God could transgress such immutable laws. Therefore, Jesus had to be divine.

But such an understanding of miracles reflects a philosophical way of thinking not quite in harmony with that of the Bible. Neither rationalists nor well-intentioned defenders of the faith have come to grips with the reality of miracles. For, without recognizing the literary and historically-conditioned context of the miracle narratives and their close association with the notion of the Kingdom of God, it is impossible to grasp the intention of the Gospel writers. Once again, we must be cautious not to impose our own concepts and interpretation upon the text, but rather to allow it to speak for itself.

THE BACKGROUND OF MIRACLES

One's opinion about miracles will depend to a great extent on how one thinks about God and the world. Popularly understood, miracles are events which surpass the laws of nature to such a degree that they must be attributed to God's intervention. But this concept of the miraculous is unknown to the biblical mind. The Bible knows nothing of nature as a closed system of "laws" which follow a constant pattern of action. In fact, the term "nature" is foreign to the biblical mentality.

In a biblical world-view, everything that happens in the realm of what we call "nature" is simply the handiwork of God. The God of Israel is recognized as living, active and very much involved with the world and the doings of his people. Israelite belief regarded all natural phenomena as the operations of a single divine being. Yahweh is the living God; he is the "Power" from whom all other manifestations of power in the universe are derived. In the Old Testament, God revealed his power especially in the realms of creation and history. No work of Yahweh is more "power-full" or "wonder-full" than his work of creation. The masterful speech from out of the whirlwind in Job, chapters 38 to 41, offers an outstanding example of the Lord's mysterious supremacy and power over nature.

As for history, the Exodus from Egypt with all of its surrounding elements — the plagues, the crossing of the Red Sea, the fall of manna in the desert — is God's greatest historical wonder or act of power in the mind of the Hebrews. The emphasis of these traditions, however, does not fall upon the "miraculous" character of the events (in fact, Hebrew has no word to translate our popular term "miracle"), but upon the "wonder" of Yahweh's power and will to save. The Israelite made no distinction between "natural" and "supernatural" happenings. Floods, earthquakes, rainbows or an unusual dryshod crossing of the "Reed" Sea (The Hebrew words that are generally translated "Red Sea" should be translated more accurately as "Reed Sea" or "Sea of Reeds." The reference is to the reeds that grow around the marshy area of Lake Timsah, a shallow extension of the Gulf of Suez), a providential supply of manna: these are all "power-full" events of a guiding and protecting God. The traditions do not exhibit a faith in "miracles," an unknown concept, but a faith in Yahweh as the Lord of nature and of history, using both to accomplish his avowed purposes.

The same thing applies to Jesus. The Gospel writers recognized him as the power of God. The wonders worked by Jesus and the apostles are generally referred to as "powers" or "works of power" (the Greek is *dunameis*, from which come the words "dynamic," "dynamo," "dynamite"). Jesus says, "If the mighty works (or "acts of power") that happened in *you* had taken place in Tyre or Sidon, they would have repented in sackcloth and ashes long ago" (Mt 11:21). Or, in another instance, witnesses of his miracles respond: "What is the wisdom given this man that such mighty works ("acts of power") should come about at his hands?" (Mk 6:2). The power of God has entered the world in the person of Jesus Christ. For this reason he is frequently hailed by the crowds as one acting with "authority," that is, with the "power" of his heavenly Father.

When we are reminded that this term "power" is used by Paul in reference to Jesus' resurrection (Rm 1:4), and for the

Gospel itself as "the power of God for the salvation of everyone who believes" (Rm 1:16), we begin to see that the biblical term for Jesus' miracles is not meant to convey primarily the spectacular or sensational, but to reflect the power of God, the theme of the Gospels. Miracles are, in a certain sense, "coming attractions" of the most prominent sign of God's power, the resurrection of Jesus. As such they are recognized only by those who see and hear by faith, a most important aspect of miracles to be discussed later in greater detail.

For the moment, we are emphasizing the historically-conditioned understanding of miracles as "acts of power" because it coheres with the Gospel concept of the emergence of God's reign into time, history and human experience. The miracles are tangible signs of God's power, signifying the overthrow of Satan and the fuller manifestation of God's sovereignty over the world. Jesus, endowed with the authority of God, enters this world enslaved by Satan, to do battle with evil. The coming of the Kingdom calls for warfare with the powers of darkness, evil and sin. The conflict is ongoing — might pitted against might — the forces of light against the powers of darkness.

MIRACLES VS. THE POWER OF EVIL

In the language and conceptuality of the first century A.D. the "works of power" performed by Jesus were seen from two dimensions: negatively, they were weapons for the overthrow of Satan and his kingdom; and positively, they revealed the healing and restoring power of God's reign. So different are these expressions from our own ways of thinking and speaking that some explanation of their historically-conditioned character is in order.

An extraordinarily strong fear of demons prevailed in the time of Jesus. All forms of disorder and chaos, be they in human beings or in nature (especially physical disorders of every conceivable kind), were attributed to malevolent powers, but most especially to the prince of evil: Satan. He appears as a commander of a military force (Lk 10:19), and even rules over a kingdom (Mt 12:26 and Lk 11:18). He is called "Beelzebub," the master of the house (Mt 10:25), who has control over his servants, the demons

(Mk 5:9). The frequent instances of demoniacal possession in the Gospel were signs of bondage to Satan and his capacity to produce disorder and chaos, the very opposite of the harmony, integrity, wholeness and "shalom" intended by God.

Jesus, endowed with the authority of his Father, comes to do battle with a world enslaved by Satan. At the very outset of his ministry, the temptation account depicted the coming of the Kingdom as a dramatic confrontation with Satan. So much of Jesus' ministry is taken up with this struggle. The many exorcisms he performed were really conflicts with evil powers. Such is the meaning of the parable of the duel: "No one can enter the strong man's house to plunder his possessions unless he first ties the strong man up; *then* he can plunder his house" (Mk 3:27). The expelling of demons was the beginning of the end, the downfall of Satan, an infallible sign of the coming of the Kingdom. "But if I drive out demons by the finger of God ("by the Spirit of God" in Mt 12:28), then the Kingdom of God has come upon you" (Lk 11:20).

Jesus then sent his disciples out to proclaim the Kingdom, and he gave them authority over the powers of evil (Lk 10:19; Mk 6:7; Mt 10:7-8). Upon returning from their mission, they reported that even demons were subject to them. And Jesus responded with joy: "I saw Satan falling like lightning from Heaven" (Lk 10:18). In other words, Jesus foresaw in the exorcisms performed by his disciples the dawn of the annihilation of Satan. The battle had already begun; victory was inevitable.

So the coming of God's reign was seen as a fight which would inevitably lead to the destruction of the Evil One. Two kingdoms are pitted against one another. Such is the logic behind Mark 3:22-27. Jesus' expulsion of demons is not a case of Satan's kingdom divided against itself, but of God's Kingdom vs. Satan's. The stronger had come to bind the weaker and to take over his dominion. The demons recognized this: "What do you want with us, Jesus of Nazareth? Have you come to destroy us? I know who you are — the Holy One of God" (Mk 1:24). Ironically, the evil spirit became an unwilling press agent of Jesus' capacity to destroy his master's kingdom and to annihilate the power of evil in every shape and form.

HEALING MIRACLES

If miracles, from one standpoint, signal the annihilation of the forces of evil, from another, Jesus' healings and cures are signs of the restoration, harmony, wholeness and reconciliation that is a part of God's reign. The two dimensions are parts of one and the same reality of the Kingdom. The dawning of God's reign is the beginning of "shalom," that fullness of relationship with God, with ourselves and with one another for which all of us are destined. The various healing miracles (expulsion of demons, the curing of epilepsy, arthritis, blindness, deafness, etc., and even the restoration of the dead to life) were tangible signs of the existence of the realm of "shalom," not some idyllic situation of the past, or a future possibility, but a present reality.

For the people of Jesus' day, not only demoniacal possession, but every disease and illness, even death itself, were attributed to the powerful bondage of Satan. According to the Old Testament ideas which they shared, all forms of sickness and suffering were the results of sin and evil. Because the biblical view of the human person does not make distinctions between body and soul, matter and spirit, all types of disorder — physical, psychological or spiritual — were simply signs of enslavement by Satan. He maintained control over the whole person. And so, to be cured, the whole person had to be freed from the power of evil. This is the idea behind Jesus' words to the paralytic (Mk 2:3-12). Before curing the man, he first says, "Your sins are forgiven." Only afterwards does he command him to stand, take up his mat and go home. The physical and the spiritual were understood as two dimensions of one and the same person.

By our standards such an explanation of evil may be inadequate. We do not generally regard the world as full of lurking spirits, maintaining a certain control or mastery over it and responsible for many of its ills and disorders. How about innocent suffering? Accidental death? There is much evil in the world that cannot be the direct result of sin. Even Jesus did not subscribe to the commonly held opinion of his time that every illness or disease was the result of personal sin (cf. Lk 13:2-5; Jn 9:3).

However, even though the reality of evil in our own times is not attributed to Satan, the understanding of evil as a power or malevolent force in the world is quite valid. One has but to scan the headlines of today's newspapers for obvious evidence of a power for evil rampant in our society. One wonders how the Gospel writers would have described the powers of violence and crime present in today's society!

By his healings and cures, Jesus was providing the power for making men and women whole and integral, for reconciling people in spirit as well as in body, for restoring harmony and order where confusion and chaos had prevailed, for initiating "shalom" in the fullest sense of that rich biblical expression. Death and illness, and even cosmic disorders, were considered part of that bondage from which only God could set people free (Lk 13:16). The question is: Does God have the power to free us from sin and evil? The response hinges on whether one can accept the reality of God's reign on earth, or not!

The annihilation of evil in whatever shape or form, physical or spiritual, involves a struggle. Even if the evil was personified in the first century, the point is that Jesus had the power to make men and women whole. In no other way was it possible to communicate such a reality except in the time-conditioned categories of that age.

For this reason, many of the miracle accounts in the Gospels include the aspect of freedom from evil as well as restoration to wholeness. When he cured those with afflictions (in Greek, the words can be translated as "scourges," "stripes," or "whips"), he was releasing them from the hold of the Evil One and making them whole again, as they were always meant to be (cf. Mk 3:10; 5:29 and Lk 7:21). To the woman cured of a severe hemorrhage, he says: "Go in *peace* ("shalom," italics mine), and be cured of your illness" (Mk 5:34). In Luke 4:39, Jesus "rebukes" or casts out a fever, much as he would rebuke or cast out a demon. Immediately, we are told, Simon's mother-in-law got up and waited on them. So completely had she been restored, that she ministered at once to the needs of her guests!

Incidentally, this double aspect of freedom from the bondage of evil and restoration to wholeness is the origin of the word "save," which may have become over-spiritualized in ordinary religious parlance. "To be saved" means not only to be freed from sin, but to be made whole once again, to be released from the realm of evil, bodily and spiritually. Being "saved" means much more than just spiritual redemption or healing. The total person is under the power of God. And so, when God saves, he touches the entire human person.

RAISING OF THE DEAD TO LIFE

One final matter remains in our consideration of healing miracles: the restoration of the dead to life. Death was Satan's ultimate stronghold. When forced to give up the realm of death, his end would be in sight. Quite apropos of this point, Paul writes to his beloved Corinthians about the meaning of Jesus' resurrection: "Christ must reign until he [God] has put all his enemies under his feet. The last enemy to be done away with will be death" (1 Cor 15:25-26). The struggle of the two kingdoms had already begun; they were locked in a titanic struggle. When death was vanquished, the Lord of Life and his realm would prevail.

For this reason, the Gospel writers attributed so much importance to the resurrection of Jesus. He overcame death, that greatest and most-feared evil, so that we might live; his resurrection was a foretaste of our future glory. Again Paul writes, "For just as in Adam all die, so too in Christ shall all be brought to life, but each one in proper order: Christ the firstfruits; then, at his coming, those who belong to [him]" (1 Cor 15:22-23).

In the raising of Jairus' daughter and the widow's son at Nain, the Gospel writers depict Jesus as the Lord of Life. He overcomes death, the strongest power of Satan. Of course, they are writing from the vantage point of the post-Easter community. They have recognized that by his resurrection and glorification, Jesus has become Lord and Messiah (Ac 2:32-33, 36; 5:31).

Accordingly, their descriptions of what actually happened in both instances are filtered through the prism of their Easter faith. Jesus has the power to restore life, as was expected in the final times announced so lyrically by the prophets of old. Not at all surprising is the reaction of the crowds in Luke's account of the widow's son (probably Luke's editorial reflection): "A great prophet has risen among us!" they said. "God has visited his people!" (Lk 7:16). As he visited Israel of old and granted it life, so now in the person of his Son, God visits his people and endows them with the fullness of life.

One might well ask at this point: "If Jesus truly shared the power of his Father to overcome evil and sin, why didn't he heal all the diseases he encountered? Why didn't he eliminate every ailment and disorder from the world?" Important here is the discussion about the Kingdom of God as "already," but "not yet." Just as the reign of God has, indeed, begun but has not yet reached full deployment, so too Christ's healing activity has broken in, but has not yet come to term. He initiated a process which is still evolving. His miracles are anticipatory signs of what the full reality will be.

Like distant lights in a far-off port, they serve as guides and offer promise of a safe haven. They indicate the final destination when "shalom" will finally be realized. In the meantime, the work of his reign continues through the efforts of his disciples. Even if little progress is apparent; even if, at times, these disciples seem to be buffeted about by contrary winds and pushed off course by opposing tides, they must still ply at the oars.

NATURE MIRACLES

Although none of the Gospel writers would have considered "nature miracles" apart from the "healing accounts," nonetheless, because of the peculiar character of these stories and the amount of embellishment and theologizing that has already surrounded them, for purposes of clarity, we prefer to treat them separately. It may be easier to understand the advent of God's reign in human experience because it involves people. But what can be said of those miracles which deal with inanimate things and with strange occurrences of nature? What is to be said of "nature miracles" like the stilling of the storm, Jesus' walk on water, his feeding of the 5,000 and the 4,000 with loaves of bread, the miraculous catch of fish, the discovery of the coin in the fish's mouth and the withering of the fig tree?

Many of these occurrences in the order of nature are not as far removed from the reality of God's reign as might first appear. The conflict between the two powers, spoken of before, extends to the cosmic order as well. So devastating is the power of sin and evil that, in a certain sense, even the world has become polluted. The flood accounts of Genesis, for example, represent the cosmic consequences of primal sin, whereby the entire known world of that time had been engulfed by the waters of chaos and disorder. The recession of the waters recall Yahweh's restoration of order and harmony to the universe, represented so graphically by the emergence of the dove with the olive branch in its bill (Gn 8:11), and the appearance of the rainbow (Gn 9:13), symbolizing a renewed covenant relationship between heaven and earth, God and humankind. As a result of sin, even material forces, once controlled by Satan, had to be won back again.

St. Paul tells us: "All creation has been groaning in labor pains up till the present" (Rm 8:22; 2 P 3:12-13). Jesus' proclamation of the Kingdom signalled a restoration of the powers of nature. So often the Messianic psalms were applied to Christ: e.g., "You have given him rule over the work of your hands, putting all things under his feet" (Ps 8:7). After all, if the Kingdom of God is, indeed, a present reality, then all of nature — animate and inanimate — is subject to his power of renewal. "Behold, I come to make all things new" is an expression that can be applied to the Risen Lord as to no other creature since the beginning of time.

A good example of a "nature miracle" is found in the stilling of the storm (Mk 4:37-41). When a raging storm threatened to capsize the boat and destroy its passengers, Jesus stood and rebuked the wind, just as he rebuked sickness or cast out demons. To the sea he says, "Silence!" or — to use a bit of colloquial language to make the point — "Shut up! Be quiet!" It was the type of personal command that he made to the demons in Mark 1:25. Then the sea became still, like someone from whom a demon had been expelled. Nature has been restored; its violent forces have been contained and tranquilized. Perhaps a similar explanation is applicable to the walking on water. In Matthew's account, at least, the miracle caused the disciples to recognize Jesus as God's Son (Mt 14:33).

But "nature miracles" have also undergone further embellishments and expansions due to the transmission of the accounts, much like the process we have already seen taking place with the parables. To convey the full Messianic significance of Jesus as the Risen Christ, the early Christian community presented the events taken from the ministry of Jesus and depicted them in terms of the fulfillment categories from the Old Testament.

For example, there are obvious points of similarity between Moses providing manna in the wilderness (Ex 16) and Jesus feeding the crowds of five thousand and four thousand in the wilderness (Mt 6:34-44; 8:1-9). The same event may also be compared with an account in 2 Kings 4:42-44 where the prophet Elisha fed a hundred people with twenty barley loaves. There are also parallels between stories where Elisha restored to life the son of a Shunamite woman (2 K 4:32-37), and where Jesus gave life back to the widow's son at Nain (Lk 7:11-17). In the Gospels, the establishment of God's reign was frequently delineated by comparing Jesus to the classic prophets of the Old Testament: Elijah, Elisha and, especially, Moses.

The present reality of God's reign, cast in prophetic categories of the past, appears in the answer given to the disciples of the Baptist (Mt 11:4-6), and shows that the miracles fulfilled Isaiah's prophecies of the days to come (Is 61:1-3; 35:5-6; 26:19). The Gospel writers did not merely cite these passages literally, but they depicted Jesus in terms of Old Testament references as the harbinger of the final times. They presented his deeds symbolically in verbal categories of fulfillment. We might protest that the events did not happen in exactly that way, but for the Gospel writers the historical Jesus who *was*, and the Christ whom they came to know in a much more profound sense after the resurrection and the coming of the Spirit, were one and the same. If they used some license in communicating his contemporary significance, it was only because they were led by the Spirit to see more about Jesus. Naturally, when it came to preaching, teaching, and catechizing, they adjusted their categories accordingly, to fit the needs of their audiences.

Some of the nature miracles were undoubtedly acted out parables. Prophets of the Old Testament spoke to their contemporaries in oral word as well as symbolic action. Isaiah walked about naked through the streets of Jerusalem to indicate the shameful depths to which Israel would fall; Jeremiah carried a wooden yoke on his shoulder to symbolize the future oppression of his people. In another incident, he smashed a clay pot in the sight of his listeners to symbolize how Yahweh would shatter his people, if they did not repent (Is 20:1-6; Jr 27:1-3; 19:1-2, 10-11, 14-15).

Similarly in the New Testament, the large catch of fish in Luke 5:1-11 was a prophetic symbolic action of how God's Word would attract future disciples; the miraculous withering of the fig tree (Mk 11:12-14; 20-25) may have been an expansion of a parable which Jesus once told about a fig tree (Lk 13:6-9), but which afterwards symbolized the rejection of Judaism due to its fruitlessness. The vinegrower came and tenderly cared for his vine, but it remained barren. Why, then, should it take up precious space and "use up the land"?

How much of this symbolic use of miracles was added by the evangelists and how much of it was part of the earliest tradition is hard to determine. But the addition of symbolism in the early Church's catechetical use of miracles is obvious in many instances. Such a symbolic interpretation is not a distortion of truth. If anything, it is an instance of effective pedagogy, intended to convey the full reality and significance of Jesus Christ to his later followers.

The Evangelists' Use of Miracles

In the transmission of the Jesus material, as we have already observed in the third chapter, the evangelists took the liberty of selecting only some of the many miracles attributed to Jesus. They ordered and arranged them into definite groups or "blocks," and then finally interpreted them to suit the needs of their audiences. Certainly, there was a change in the form and content of the accounts, but no one ever considered this a distortion of the original, or a lack of fidelity in transmitting what Jesus had actually done. For them, the power of God revealed in the miracles of Jesus was ongoing; it continued to be effective through the Spirit and Word, now proclaimed through the evangelists. Death did not eliminate Jesus totally from the historical scene because, by his resurrection and sending of the Spirit, he continued to touch and heal his disciples in a new way.

A particularly striking example of this process appears in Matthew's account of the stilling of the storm (8:23-27). The entire context of the scene is permeated with the themes of "following and discipleship" (cf. Mt 8:18-22, the difficulties of discipleship: no place to lay your head, no family to call your own; nonetheless (8:23), "when he got into the boat, the disciples followed him"). A close comparison of these passages describing the storm at sea (Mk 4:35-41 and Lk 8:22-25) shows how Matthew has subtly, but ingeniously, transformed the scene to apply to the disciples of his own community, who were encountering new crises and problems some forty or fifty years after the original event. Instead of the ordinary word for "storm" used by Mark and Luke, Matthew uses a word which describes the "apocalyptic" storm which will one day sweep over the whole world. He changed the order of the account. Where Mark and Luke have the stilling of the storm first, then the words of Jesus, Matthew highlights the words of Jesus demanding faith. For him this is important, even more so, than the actual stilling of the sea.

The most striking change, however, is the response of the disciples:

Mk 4:38 "Teacher, doesn't it matter to you that we're going to die?"
Lk 8:24 "Master, master, we're going to die!"
Mt 8:25 "Lord, save us, we're going to die!"

The latter address: "Lord, save us!" is one which Christians frequently used in worship, a post-Easter expression of prayerful exhortation. When we recall that from the earliest times the ship was a symbol of the Christian Church, then we begin to appreciate Matthew's application of the account. The scene has shifted from an incident in the life of Jesus to the context of the Church in

Matthew's time, depicted as a storm-tossed ship buffeted about by the winds of conflict and crisis. Matthew's community, fearful, frightened and waning in faith, is reminded of the words of the Lord — as valid then as when they were first spoken — "Why are you afraid, O you of little faith?" Addressed first to those disciples who were just beginning to believe, now they are addressed to later disciples who had to be encouraged to persevere in a faith already established but beginning to wane. A miracle performed by Jesus during his lifetime thus became a lesson in discipleship for the Christian community of Matthew's time, well after the death and resurrection of Jesus.

To summarize: the Synoptic Gospels present the miracles as signs of the advent of God's reign into time, history and human experience. Jesus reveals the power of God in the world, and his miracles are signs of the effectual working out of that power. As a foreshadowing of the coming reign of God, indeed already realizing it, people are being freed from the bonds of Satan, sins are forgiven, demons driven out, paralytics and cripples are made whole. These miracles can only mean one thing: that One stronger than Satan has taken the field. Now is the beginning of the end of all that pertains to the realm of evil. The Kingdom of God is at hand!

Not only do miracles signify the coming of the reign, but they also demonstrate the manner in which this happens. Where God exercises his reign, people are healed both physically and spiritually; they are "saved," i.e., they are made whole. The "whole person" shares in God's peace, that quality which makes them integral in their relationship with God, with themselves and with one another.

The primitive understanding of miracles as expressive of the reign of God was later expanded further within the growing consciousness of the Church to express symbolically the nature and demands of the Kingdom, especially in relationship to the Old Testament.

The Purpose of Miracles

Thus the purpose of Gospel miracles was not to portray Jesus as the most sensational wonder worker of all times. Nor was it the primary intent of the Gospel writers to present him as an outstanding humanitarian or a uniquely compassionate person, though the latter virtues are not lacking in their descriptions.

Neither were miracles intended to prove the divinity of Jesus. The apologetic manuals of the past which tried to prove the divinity of Jesus from miracles were based upon an erroneous understanding of miracles as happenings surpassing the laws of nature. But this definition does not harmonize with the biblical concept of miracles, as we have already seen.

Furthermore, one cannot *prove* that an occurrence is an act of God; only faith can recognize it as such. We cannot prove the divinity of Jesus by an occurrence which can be seen for what it is only by an act of faith. Otherwise, one runs into a vicious circle. Miracles are not proofs; they are challenges to faith. They are signs of God's presence and activity in the deeds of Jesus. And this leads us logically to a consideration of another very important aspect of miracles.

Miracles and Faith

The element of faith was intrinsic to Jesus' miracles. Faith is associated with the character of miracles as signs. But signs attain their full meaning only when understood correctly. The miracles of Jesus, however, were variously interpreted. Whatever took place was not so absolutely convincing and evocative of God's presence and activity to the degree that it would *compel* immediate recognition and assent on the part of a witness. Otherwise, why is it that so few believed? What happened to all the others? Were they all blind and hard-of-heart?

There were, after all, charlatans and frauds who attributed to themselves incredible powers. In fact, the scribes and Pharisees accused Jesus of performing signs by the power of Beelzebub (Mk 3:22; Mt 12:24-28), not by the power of God. In the ancient world, pagans told of miracles performed by Simon the Sorcerer (Ac 8:9-24), and by a wandering Pythagorean philosopher, Apollonius of Tyana. There are also stories about certain renowned rabbis who were said to have performed miracles. In other words, the miracles of Jesus must be called ambiguous, because in the atmosphere of that time, others were said to have performed "miracles." Thus they could be interpreted in various ways. Jesus possessed an unusual authority. But whose was it? There is a choice involved: one can confess miracles to be acts of God, or explain them in some other way.

There are, of course, major differences between the sober, unpretentious character of the Gospel miracle-narratives and the frequently sensational and often bizarre character of the extrabiblical accounts. For example, a miracle recorded at Epidaurus in Greece relates the case of a woman who, after a pregnancy of five years, gave birth to a four-year-old son!

Brevity precludes the possibility of further discussion about the difference between such extrabiblical accounts and Gospel miracles. For the moment, we are trying to emphasize the quality of faith involved, because there are certain important factors to be considered in the relationship between miracles and faith.

Faith, as we have said, is intrinsic to the recognition of miracles as signs of God's activity. For example, because Jesus found no faith in his hometown of Nazareth, he was unable to perform any miracles there (Mk 6:5). After several healings, Jesus says: "Go your way, your faith has saved you" (Mk 10:52). When Peter tried to follow Jesus by walking on water (Mt 14:28), he became frightened and began to sink. Jesus stretched out his hand and caught him. "O you of little faith, why did you doubt?" he exclaimed. To recognize Jesus, and then to follow him, demands faith!

One has only to read carefully through the miracle narratives in Matthew (chapters 8 and 9) to notice how the descriptive aspects of the miracles are greatly subdued when compared with parallel passages in Mark and Luke. Matthew concentrates on the dialogue between the recipient of the miracle and Jesus. The dialogue always centers on the need for faith.

Faith is the context in which God's power comes to fruition, and this power is thwarted by unbelief (Mk 6:5-6; Mt 17:19-20). Faith allows for degrees, varying from initial trust in Jesus' power to a more assured belief in the full significance of his person. But faith is never something completed, an accomplished fact; it is ever becoming, growing, deepening. The ideal attitude is that of the father of the boy with epilepsy: "I believe; help my unbelief!" (Mk 9:24). Jesus did not first demand acknowledgment of himself as God's Son before performing a miracle; he required that kind of faith which remained open to the possibility of further growth and development, but a faith that represented at least a readiness to accept the reality of God's presence and activity.

Thus anyone who accepts the miracles of Jesus as signs assumes a risk. The risk is one of discipleship, of recognizing that in this particular event God is at work; not a human being, not sorcery, not Satan. For the Gospel writers, miracles were effective signs of God's activity, and of the present reality of his reign. If we cannot accept their interpretation, the only other alternative is skepticism. If the miracles are an essential part of the preaching of Christianity, then we are confronted with the question of whether the power of God was revealed in Jesus or not. Each one of us is confronted with a decision: yes or no?

No one can stand on the side-lines like an impartial observer. Everyone who approaches the Gospels is either a believer, even if only incipiently, or an unbeliever. One cannot recognize a miracle as the power of God unless there is belief. One cannot treat miracles scientifically, like experiments in physics or chemistry which will yield certain critically-ascertainable results if all the requirements are fulfilled. No amount of critical biblical investigation will prove that miracles are acts of God, even if they are analyzed, surgically dissected with the scalpel of literary and historical criticism, and then meticulously laid out and studied by the sharp eye of a scholar. It's been tried all too often and failed! No matter how far back we probe to the original event, at bed-rock we are confronted with a nucleus of tradition which does not allow further dissection, where fact and interpretation are already wedded. This is where the challenge of faith comes in. Only those with faith understood the true meaning of the miracles and accepted the significance of the message. Others also saw, but could not believe. They had no faith.

Consider the example of a passerby who chances upon a horrendous car accident. The wreckage is so total that any chance of an occupant's survival seems impossible. Suddenly, incredibly, the driver, the sole occupant of the car, crawls out of the mass of bent steel and emerges safe and unharmed. The passerby helps him and says, "You certainly were lucky to have come out of that alive! I don't know how you managed it!"

The survivor, on the other hand, in his heart truly believes that he has been spared by the provident hand of God and exclaims, "Thanks be to God! It was a miracle!" Two witnesses to the same spectacular event: one judges it to be luck, the other attributes it to the provident hand of God. Granted, there are obvious limitations to such an example. There was a certain uniqueness to the acts performed by Jesus of Nazareth which is not quite the case in the car accident. And yet we may learn from it. There were those who "saw" certain signs performed by Jesus, yet could not believe. Maybe they thought he was a magician, a charlatan or a fake. Yet there were others who also "saw," and who did believe. These recognized that Jesus was, indeed, acting by the power of God.

So the answer to the question, "Did the miracles actually happen?" is always a personal one. This does not imply, however, a purely private interpretation of the text. After all, to understand the mind of the first century writers, one must avail oneself of the tools and techniques available to clarify the context and words of a given passage. For this reason, no historian, scientist, biblical scholar or Church authority can answer the question in such a totally convincing manner that one would be *forced* to believe. At most, biblical scholarship can tell us that the Gospel writers truly believed the miracles did happen, and this belief is rooted in the historical Jesus. But then the rest remains to us. We have to take that final leap: "Yes, Lord, I do believe, but help my unbelief."

Frequently we look to authority to give us the answers that only we can make. That may be a cop-out on our part. It's always easier to have someone else make the decision and to assure us that miracles did, indeed, happen. However, even after the most detailed explanations of the Gospel text, we are ultimately confronted with a decision which only we can make. The answer is, in the final analysis, a personal one. It is the "yes" of faith which confronts each and every one of us when we come up against the person of Jesus Christ.

MIRACLES IN OUR LIVES

Miracles tell us that God's power is a present reality, not only in time and history, but also in our very own human experience. Incredible as it may seem, Jesus transferred this same power and authority to his disciples. He gave them the mandate to continue his mission, and to proclaim for all times the reality of God's reign (Lk 10:9 ff.). His followers recognized that they were so endowed, and ratified this power by performing many signs and wonders recorded in the earliest history of the Church, the Acts of the Apostles. With the coming of the Holy Spirit, the continued presence of the Lord and his power would be assured in his community until the end of time (Mt 28:16-20).

Now the Kingdom is evidenced in the efforts of Jesus' disciples to annihilate evil, to overcome sin and selfishness, to heal and to restore, to reconcile people to God and to work for harmony and peace in their relationships with one another. In spite of professing the reality of God's reign in our human experience, in practice, we do sometimes give the impression of having an unearthly and unreal understanding of this reality. For so many of us, miracles are still extraordinary events, unique happenings, seldom experienced in life. While the Jesus-event was a unique, once-and-for-all happening, it would be a mistake to relegate miracles only to the cures attached to special places like Lourdes, Fatima, Medjugorje, or even to some exceptional instances of healing recorded from time to time.

There are less pretentious, ordinary, down-to-earth instances of healing that take place daily, if only we have the eyes of faith to perceive them, and to recognize that we also have the power to perform them. We refer again to the full meaning of the biblical term, "shalom" — peace. The Kingdom of God is a present reality when "shalom" is vital and dynamic. Peace in its profound biblical sense means harmony, integrity, wholeness. When we are in a harmonious relationship with God, when we recognize the incredible gift of grace that we share as daughters and sons of God in and through our brother Jesus Christ, when we allow ourselves to be guided by the Spirit of the Risen Lord, then we are not only in harmony with the Triune God, but with ourselves, with others and with the whole created world. This is the true inner peace that leads to freedom. Such an experience of wholeness and peace is what it means to be "saved." It is based upon the faithful "yes" that one says to the reality of the Kingdom as experienced now.

If the Spirit of the Risen Lord continues to act in his Church, the Body of Christ, in his community of believers, in his disciples, then miracles are possible today. Whenever we work to make people whole in the name of Jesus, whenever we make others aware of the fatherhood of God and the brotherhood of Jesus and the powerful indwelling of the Holy Spirit, miracles are happening. Whenever we touch others with understanding and love, whenever we heal the spiritually fragmented and maimed, whenever we open the eyes of the blind and unstop the ears of the deaf with the word of the Lord, miracles are happening. When we expend our energies to eradicate bigotry, hatred, prejudice and war, whenever we help men and women realize their common fraternity in Christ, miracles are happening. Whenever we strive to establish this harmony with God and one another through the particular vocation or ministry we possess, miracles are happening. Then the signs of God's Kingdom are again present in our midst. Then Christ is recognizable in the world. He is acting through his Spirit, but in us, his disciples. Then those who have eyes to see and ears to hear will recognize the reality of God's reign on earth. Then the world will know that God is still alive, because of the clear signs of his presence in those who dare call themselves his followers. Are miracles still possible? It all depends on us. If we, as Christians, really believe, then we will make them happen.

QUESTIONS FOR DISCUSSION

1. What is your understanding of "miracle"? Does it differ from the understanding of miracles described in this chapter?

2. How is the power of evil most evident in today's society? Who is responsible for it?

3. Where is the power of healing, restoration and reconciliation most evident in our times?

4. Do symbolic actions, like those of the prophets and Jesus (e.g., the withering of the fig tree) have any significance today? Can you give some examples?

5. What is the difference between a miracle and some unusual or unexpected occurrence? Can you give some examples?

6. How do you understand the "risk" of Christianity in your own personal life?

7. Are you aware of "miracles" happening in your life? Can you give some examples?

8. How would you convey the reality of miracles to a group of youngsters? Or teenagers?

CHAPTER VII

THE KINGDOM ETHIC

Mark 12:28-34;   Matthew 5 - 7; 19:16-30; 22:34-40;
Luke 6:17-49; 10:25-37

The parables and miracles of Jesus proclaim a single theme: the coming of the Kingdom. God's entrance into time, history and human experience in the person of his Son, Jesus Christ, offers men and women an invitation to a new way of life and a new relationship with himself.

But an invitation demands a response. The parables of Jesus called forth genuine joy, a spirit of forgiveness and reconciliation, a radically new orientation to God and people, a concern for others in need, a complete trust in the future and in God. Miracles also confronted Jesus' disciples with a challenge of faith in the reality of God's power made present once again. They were authorized to continue performing "acts of power": to destroy the realm of evil, to heal and to restore "shalom," and to continue the mission of building the Kingdom which he had initiated.

The moral teaching of the first three Gospels is fundamentally a "Kingdom ethic." It illustrates the type of response which individuals must make to share in this radically new relationship. It's the qualitative response that is expected of each person who has said "yes" to the reality of the Kingdom. The manner in which we respond will determine the quality of our discipleship. Some further background will be necessary, however, to help us appreciate the full implications of the "Kingdom way" and the possibilities it offers the contemporary Christian.

97

Confused Moral Situation of Today

In our own times, a rapidly changing cultural situation has spawned new ideologies, new conceptions of God and humankind, new behavioral patterns, so that a certain confusion and uncertainty has set in concerning traditional Christian moral teaching. Children come home from school today and, to the shock and disbelief of their parents, begin recounting the "new ideas" proposed by their teachers or which are circulating among their peers: missing Mass on Sunday may not be seriously sinful; "love" and "respect" for one another are the only necessary ingredients in boy-girl relationships; mortal sins are committed rarely and with difficulty. There is much talk about the "law of love," the need to follow one's own conscience, personal fulfillment and the importance of fundamental options.

Parents, quite understandably, are upset, perplexed and have difficulty adjusting to these "new ideas," some of which are erroneous, while others represent newer trends in moral theology. Churches are experiencing an increasingly waning adherence to their long-standing ethical systems. Teachers of religion are frustrated by the unwillingness of students to accept, or even listen to, traditional moral values. Was the moral teaching of the past all that bad? Where does one turn today to find out what is right and what is wrong? What did Jesus teach about moral behavior? Even if a comprehensive ethical system based on the Gospels is not possible (for reasons to be seen later), perhaps a deeper understanding and response to the demands of Jesus will offer a sane corrective and much-needed balance to the present confused state of Christian morality.

The reasons behind the changes in moral attitudes today are many and complex. A brief discussion like this will hardly do justice to the varied cultural, ideological and historical factors which influence change in moral behavior. However, one aspect which enters prominently into our consideration is the divorce between morality and God's revelation in the Scriptures.

For too long, moral theology, the discipline which applies God's teaching to moral behavior, was dissociated from the Bible. It had become a separate discipline, an entity unto itself, an elaborate system of laws and directives which at times lacked a solid biblical foundation. Some of this was due, no doubt, to the attempt on the part of moral theologians to provide priests with a complete system for judging sins in the confessional. The result was a science for the confessional, a handbook for determining the number and species of sin, but a process which, unfortunately, all too often led to a negative and legalistic approach to morality. Moral theology, separated from the "good news" of Jesus, forgot the initiating action of God and tended to emphasize the non-performance or failure of the sinner. The result was a juridical type of approach which tended to place a heavy stress on the external features of the law, while often disregarding the meaning behind the law. Moral teaching gave the impression of being a system of do's and don'ts, with emphasis upon the latter. When solidly founded upon God's revelation in the Bible, however, Christian moral life is seen as the human response to the saving word and work of God in Jesus Christ.

God did not reveal a code of morality or a detailed ethical system; God's was a *self*-revelation. Biblical morality, a fundamental norm for a broader Christian morality, must be seen, therefore, in terms of a qualitative personal response to God's revelation of himself as a person. The stress is on the total person with all of his or her basic relationships, and the fundamental option that he or she has made for Kingdom values, instead of a harping on individual external acts. In individual instances we can fall, and fall badly, without thereby immediately condemning ourselves.

The scriptural approach emphasizes the primacy of responsible action, instead of a niggardly performance of do's and an avoidance of don'ts. More emphasis is given to conversion, that radical change of mind and heart, indeed of the whole person who is confronted with the reality of God's reign. Furthermore, the tension that exists in a disciple who has confronted the "already" of God's reign, but who also perceives the "not yet," brings out so much more the fragile nature of a sinful person and the context of the "world" in which he or she lives. Needed attention is given to the long process of growth and development in an individual's moral response, the continual adjustment to changing cultural circumstances and the importance of taking into account the innumerable social influences which condition a modern person's acts.

Thus if "new ideas" are being proposed, if there is need for a reevaluation of our traditional moral teaching, we must ultimately be guided by the full dimension of God's revelation and its ongoing interpretation within the Church, namely, the process of tradition. Scriptural norms, once ascertained and properly interpreted, must then be applied by the Church, the teacher of morals, to the historical and cultural circumstances of today's believer.

Before we get too far ahead of ourselves, we will first survey briefly some of the principal features of Israel's moral response to God in the Old Testament. If Jesus inherited a certain understanding of the Law from his Jewish tradition, how did he interpret it? Did he abolish it, or did he restore some of the values it had lost?

PRINCIPAL FEATURES OF OLD TESTAMENT MORALITY

The Christian cannot look at "law" in the Old Testament apart from the interpretation given by Jesus. His viewpoint has been enshrined in the classic words of Matthew 5:17: "Don't think that I came to destroy the Torah or the Prophets; I came not to destroy, but to fulfill." But what "law" is to be fulfilled? And how is it to be fulfilled?

Law in the Old Testament must always be seen as *torah*, not as a system of legal formulations or directives but, as the Hebrew word suggests, guidance, teaching, or even instruction in the way of life. The Israelites associated *torah* with life, the way one conducts oneself in life with all of its vital relationships. Interestingly, the first five books of the Bible are popularly referred to as Torah, because they were looked upon as a law, a rule, an authoritative guide for one's life, a way of life.

The means or the approach used to express God's moral will toward his people was the covenant: a bond, a pact between two people, modeled broadly on the agreements made between Oriental sovereigns and their subjects. But God's covenant made with his chosen people was unique. Initiated by a gracious gift of election, it demanded a response of fidelity and love. Israel affirmed its unique relationship with Yahweh by recalling that common refrain: "I am your God, and you are my people."

Israelite law must always be seen in light of this unique covenant relationship. The Ten Commandments, for example, are simply Israel's response to this unique relationship, the stipulations to be carried out by a covenant partner. The Hebrew refers to them as the "ten words" of response because they suggest a dialogue which obliges the Israelite to a special way of life, the covenant way, the qualitative response made to a gracious God by a faithful covenant partner. The emphasis is always on the need for heart and inner motivation instead of a mere external compliance to the law.

The purpose of the law, then, was to give external expression to the reality of the covenant. But implied always was heart and inner motivation, without which a commitment of service — even of a chosen people — could become sterile. The qualitative response sought was not one of pure justice, but a freely-willed, personal and generous response, like that between lovers. That very same idea is conveyed by the prophets when they appealed for *hesed*, a term loosely translated as "steadfast love" or "covenant loyalty," the free, generous act of self-giving that betokens the affection between lover and loved one.

Detached from the covenant, as happened in later Judaism, the law became a dead letter, empty and void. It became an end in itself, instead of a basis for loyal response. Without heart, a law can become cold and mechanical; response becomes perfunctory and quickly degenerates into formalism. A good portion of the prophetic indictment of Israel was occasioned precisely by such a loveless performance of the *torah*, a purely external response that fulfilled the letter but lacked the inner spirit. No surprise then that the prophets frequently spoke of sin in terms of "treachery" or "infidelity," and compared it to the action of an unfaithful marriage partner, because the violation was not merely that of a law or an external prescription, but an unwillingness to respond freely, faithfully and spontaneously with self-giving love.

The same idea is applicable to our own times. It's not the memorization of the Ten Commandments that is of primary

importance, but living out their meaning and the inner relationship which they imply. While there is nothing wrong with memo-
rizing the Commandments, such an act in itself does not necessarily make a good Christian, or a good Jew for that matter. What
does matter is the genuine motivation prompted by a grateful
heart.

The cult of the law developed to such a degree in later
Judaism that it became a "fence" (a "hedge" as it was called by the
Jews), consisting of countless legal opinions, which advanced the
obligations of the law beyond the sense of the words, and thus
made it exceedingly difficult to violate. The law, as a result,
became an end in itself; strict and punctilious performance of the
law became the trademark of good moral behavior. Rigid observance of the law separated pious Jews from all other "outsiders."
The law became a badge of identity, a wall of separation. The
negative effect of such a "fence" around the law created the
impression that mere legal observance was all that was necessary
to serve God and to be a loyal Jew.

Such was not the attitude of Jesus. He was not opposed to the
law. He came not to annul the law, but to fulfill it. So insistent was
he on this point, as a matter of fact, that he would not allow entry
into the Kingdom of God without observance of the law (Mt 5:19-
20). But he did reject the law as an end in itself; he rejected that
straining for minute observance of "every jot and tittle," while
disregarding the heart and a genuinely motivated response. For
the law of itself is an insufficient means of reaching God; it must
reach its fullness in him. Conversion to the reign of God is the only
way of attaining that fullness. And here lies the central moral
message of the Gospels as preached by Jesus.

Gospel morality must always be seen in the context of the
Kingdom of God. It is intimately connected with what has already
been said about parables and miracles and our experience when
confronted by them. Jesus' ethic is for "Kingdom people." It's the
"Kingdom way" of living: a certain attitude and outlook that one
projects into the daily task of living which is based on a personal
relationship to God in Christ and through his Spirit with one
another.

What this "Kingdom way" calls for in terms of human

response is not spelled out in detail. The Gospels offer general principles, maxims, sayings and examples which illustrate the very high level of the ideals presented by Jesus. They tell us how far we should reach — extremely high: "So *you* be perfect as your Heavenly Father is perfect" (Mt 5:48). Even if we are not told *how* such ideals are to be attained, even if our life circumstances are very different from those in which they were first spoken, nonetheless they do spell out sufficient norms, a general direction, a way to be followed by disciples of all generations.

THE ETHIC OF JESUS
BASED ON THE KINGDOM OF GOD

A recalling of the conclusions made in the first three chapters will be extremely beneficial at this point. Failure to recognize the complex character of the Gospels and their long process of growth and development can easily lead to a simplistic and naïve understanding of Gospel morality. Because the Gospels are not biographies or strict histories of Jesus, but the written testimony of the faith and experiences of the earliest disciples, the discovery and understanding of the moral teaching of Jesus becomes more difficult for today's readers. Before proceeding, certain presuppositions must be taken into account:

1. Those sayings that call for a moral response are scattered throughout the Gospel in seeming disarray. The Gospel writers had no intention of leaving for future generations a systematic textbook of morality, a categorical listing of virtues and vices, or some kind of an ethical code of conduct to guide Church authorities. Neither is the content of the Gospels so comprehensive that it even pretends to cover every moral topic. Many of the complex moral situations confronting today's society were hardly envisioned by writers in their first century Palestinian setting. The morality of mercy-killing, abortion, genetic manipulation, invasion of personal rights by government, nuclear war, environmental issues and other contemporary problems were never even dreamed of by the Gospel writers.

Even when Jesus does allude to a moral response, there is an "occasional" nature about these allusions; they are not gathered comprehensively in any one section for future reference. Often they consist of single, isolated sentences given without a context, "floating maxims and sayings." Sometimes these sayings are found in different contexts in different Gospels. The preached word was dynamic and alive. A strong consciousness of the continued presence of the Lord in his word allowed for a rather flexible application to different needs and circumstances. Occasionally, the evangelists would group the various sayings together into a collection, or arrange them into categories around a single theme, e.g., "righteousness" in the Sermon on the Mount (Mt 5:20).

2. Because these occasional sayings of Jesus were subject to a long process of transmission from an oral stage to gradual fixation in written form, and ultimately to the final composition by the evangelists (Chapters 1-3), there is every probability that the sayings were revised, reinterpreted, and re-adapted to new audiences all along the line. Since Jesus did not respond to all of the moral problems facing the later Church, his followers had to appeal to the mind of the Master and then interpret, adapt and apply it to new situations. Those responsible for preaching and teaching his words did so, not woodenly, but in an existential manner, because they were strongly conscious of the continued presence of the Lord in his community (Mt 28:16-20).

3. Because our discussion of the moral teaching of Jesus will rely on the first three Gospels only, the conclusions will be somewhat restricted. Obviously, a more comprehensive coverage of the topic would have to include the Gospel of John, the letters of Paul, the Pastoral Epistles and the other New Testament literature. Why? Because each writer betrays a distinctive brand of moral response, reflecting the specific application he makes of the new life of Christ to the differing needs of his audiences.

Jesus did not leave for posterity a clearly formulated code of morality, only the example of his person, the tradition of his words and the memory of his deeds. Understandably, new moral problems and ethical situations developed after his departure, all of which called for new decisions. The followers of Jesus found themselves giving moral interpretations on issues for which Jesus gave no specific ruling. They were following his mind, his attitudes, the tenor and direction of his words. They tried to recall what he had said about the "Kingdom way." For this reason, we make no attempt here to try and give a full picture of the moral teaching of Jesus. At best, we can offer a few important characteristics of what may be called, for lack of a better word, a "Kingdom morality."

What is the "Kingdom way"? What is characteristic of the moral response demanded of a disciple of the Kingdom? What is essential in the behavioral patterns of one who is called to accept the reality of God's reign? If the "following of Christ" is an appropriate expression for the lifestyle of a believing Christian, what is the direction or way one follows in the footsteps of the Master?

Some Characteristics of "Kingdom Morality"

Certain characteristics of the reign of God will bring out the distinctiveness of Gospel morality: 1. God's gift. 2. Conversion. 3. The implications of the "already" and the "not yet" of the Kingdom.

First, Gospel morality is always set in the context of Grace. In other words, the reality of God's reign in human experience is divinely initiated; it is God's gift to us, not our gift to God (cf. the parables of the tenants and the wedding banquet, Mt 21:33-22:10). There are no purely human formulas, ethical guidelines, blueprints for moral living that will lead us with assurance to the divine. It is more true to say that God saves us in spite of ourselves, in spite of our blindness and hardness of heart, in spite of our shabby response. We can only respond freely, personally and genuinely to God's gracious gift. Otherwise, we fall into the error of thinking that we become moral by our own resources and talents. But we do not save ourselves. When we start imposing our own standards, our own criteria for moral behavior, when we start measuring how much is demanded, how far we can go without committing sin, the result is a negative, juridical and overly-legalistic morality.

When a spirit of legalism besets morality, laws are multiplied, subdivided and neatly categorized. But, paradoxically, while imposing heavy burdens, the law does not ask too much of people, but too little. The temptation arises of doing the minimum, instead of striving for the maximum. Merely fulfilling the letter of the law can lead to a certain smugness, self-sufficiency and pride that ignores the need for God. Jesus categorically rejected such an attitude. In fact, it was precisely such a mental disposition that blinded the scribes and Pharisees to the reality of God's reign (cf. Mt 23). Jesus came bearing God's gift which promised a level of life that human beings alone could not possibly attain. His Kingdom message was, in fact, an invitation to become more "perfect" in imitation of the perfection exemplified by Jesus himself: "So *you* be perfect as your Heavenly Father is perfect" (Mt 5:48).

Secondly, the basic response for people of the Kingdom presupposes "conversion," that joyful change of heart and acceptance of the gift of God in Jesus Christ (cf. Chapter 4). Conversion is fundamental to the preaching of Jesus about the reign of God: "The proper time has been fulfilled and the Kingdom of God has come; repent and believe in the good news" (Mk 1:15; cf. also Mt 4:17; Lk 4:43). Without conversion not only belief in the "good news," but any type of inner motivation and heart so requisite for genuine moral response is impossible. It implies the reality, the power, and the universality of sin, and the genuine, entire and interior change of belief and attitude which is necessary to escape from sin and turn to the ways of God. It is by change of heart that a person becomes a friend of God and a recipient of divine life.

Conversion is more than a heightened intellectual awareness or an overwhelming emotional experience resulting from a dramatic and personal confrontation with the reality of Jesus Christ, although these are not precluded. Conversion really means a radical transformation of oneself, resulting in a new way of life founded upon the radical demands of the Gospel. The stress is on "radical," not in the sense of revolutionary — though conversion does result in an inner revolution which must have ramifications in the order of society — but in the sense of being rooted in the person and demands of Christ.

Conversion is relational. It is founded upon a new relationship between God and humankind, and between men and women with one another. The life offered by the Father in the person of his Son and communicated through the action of the Holy Spirit is received in faith and practiced in love. Love is merely "lived faith." Once transformed, we return God's gift through love of neighbor in the "sacrament of the neighbor." But more about the ethic of love later, for now we must consider the final characteristic of "Kingdom morality."

Third, a tension exists in the person who has experienced the "already" of the reign of God but who has also recognized a "not yet" still to be realized. If God's reign is a present reality, then the radical conversion process of a disciple must take place in this world, in the midst of a sinful and unredeemed people, in a specific culture and environment and in very existential day-to-day circumstances. In other words, conversion is realized in the material and worldly aspects of life. A Christian's attitude toward the world cannot be one of flight or renunciation.

Sometimes "Kingdom of God" is regarded as a quaint biblical expression of an age long past, without taking seriously the present reality of the Kingdom in our times, in our history, and in our own human experience. Many Christians have a built-in fear of the world, an excessive fear of its snares and wiles, an attitude not quite consistent with a disciple's responsibility of constantly working to overcome the powers of evil. If the invitation to the Kingdom is made *now*, I can't renege. I can't be biding my time, patiently waiting for the final coming of the Lord. I can't be waiting for heaven. Heaven, in a certain sense, has already begun on earth (and hell may also have begun here, too!). Cooperation with the grace of the Kingdom is a *now* obligation. There is much work to be done... now.

The attitude of some Christians betrays a desire, even if only implicitly, to get away from the monotony and drabness of the normal day-to-day circumstances of life, and to do God's work in some quiet, secluded enclosure. "If only I had the peace and quiet to give myself totally and unreservedly to God's work!" But such an attitude underrates the value of the world; it reflects an exaggerated glorification of the contemplative. And, above all, it may be somewhat unreal. Sometimes Christians find it hard to believe that in the drab routine of daily living the reign of God is present and active. Like it or not, our home, our neighbor, our community, our cities, our nation is where God's action is taking place, and where believers are expected to respond.

God's reign also has social and cosmic dimensions. Human conversion is relational. The relationship between God and ourselves is not a private relationship. It implies a new attitude, a new outlook and a new vision regarding people and society. How could one ever speak of building the Kingdom of God on earth, of bringing about a "new heaven and a new earth," and at the same time close one's eyes to the reality of poverty, hatred, bigotry, prejudice, violence and the endless litany of disorder and evil? How could one ever speak of the values of the Kingdom in the face of injustice, gross materialism and secularism? How could we ever forget that the betterment of the world and human society is a promotion of the reign of God? If we are believers, who are convinced of the present reality of God's reign, we can't run from the world, we can't hide, we can't deny or gloss over the forces of evil, but we must do something about them. We must respond... the Kingdom way.

But there is also the "not yet" of the Kingdom. The call to prompt and decisive action in our present times and circumstances must also be realistic. The Kingdom, while present, has a future dimension. Conversion is not a static, once-and-for-all process; it is continuous, developing, ever becoming. The powers of evil are well entrenched and do not yield easily. In spite of our best efforts, we are still sinful and selfish. The future element of the Kingdom suggests the need for continued growth and conversion.

We can't ever think we "have it made"! We can't ever be duped into thinking that Utopia lies ahead, that short-term progress and achievements are permanent. We are always trying to overcome selfishness. We are a community of the redeemed, but also a Church of sinners. In the Risen Lord, the victory has already been assured, but there are still many battles to be fought. We pray daily: "Lead us not into temptation, but deliver us from evil (the Evil One)." The petition is a plea for strength during those inevitable crises to come, and for freedom from the powers of Satan (the Evil One). A titanic struggle with Satan stands between the "already" of the Kingdom and its "not yet" to be realized at some future period.

The formulators of the documents of the Second Vatican Council, speaking of this unrealized, future aspect of the Church, very appropriately termed it a "pilgrim Church": a people on the way, redeemed but sinful, victorious but still ready to do battle, a Church reformed but still in need of reformation, a community with its destination marked but still in the wilderness. Such is the tension that is part of a Christian who responds fully to the "already" of God's reign, but is aware that he or she must still struggle and pray for the "not yet" — the full realization to take place in God's good time.

An Ethic of Love

To discuss the moral teaching of Jesus is impossible without discussing the centrality of love. The commandment of love of God is called the "greatest" (Mt 22:34-40), or the "first" (Mk 12:28-31), or the commandment by which one attains eternal life (Lk 1:25-28). Matthew adds further that the entire law and the prophets — the entire revelation made to Israel — depends on these two commandments (Mt 22:40; cf. Rm 13:8-10).

The unique interpretation given by Jesus to the love commandment was his insistence on the interior bond between love of God and love of people. They are not two loves, but one. What is done to one's neighbor is done to Christ (Mt 25:40-45). In the final judgment scene depicted by Matthew (25:31-46), the entire assembly is divided into two groups solely on the basis of the service they have rendered to others. Love is the fulfillment of the law and the basis for eternal life; the absence of love is eternal condemnation.

While commandments such as those which prohibit murder, adultery and injustice are not voided, it is fairly certain that those who love their neighbor genuinely will not commit these crimes; they will not sin.

An important aspect of the commandment of love, one which literally pushes a disciple to the furthest limits, is the love even of one's enemies (Mt 5:43-48). While John's Gospel tells us that a Christian cannot prove his love for God except through the love of neighbor, Matthew claims that it is not really proved unless the person loved is an enemy. Incredible! While reason might demand moderation in love of all things, faith destroys moderation and bases Christian love for others on the love Jesus had for us: selfless, gratuitous, in no way depending on human qualities and response. The enemy can give the lover nothing in return; if anything, hatred. Christ's love is universal; the criterion is need, so poignantly illustrated in the parable of the Good Samaritan (Lk 10:29-37).

There is, of course, a world of difference between loving an enemy and liking him. Loving a murderer, a kidnapper or an abortionist may be emotionally impossible. The Christian loves his enemies as Christ loved sinners. Like Jesus, Christians are to be agents of forgiveness and reconciliation; to be just but merciful; to be persevering in their determination to bring their enemies to the full realization of truth and love. Admittedly, not an easy task!

No one will deny the difficulties which arise in trying to reduce these high ideals to ethical formulas. Loving God and neighbor is an extremely high ideal; even more challenging is the love of enemies. How does one ever formulate and systematize ideals into specific laws and regulations? Smothering the love commandment with a mountain of rules and specifications stifles free, spontaneous and generous response. On the other hand, sinful and unredeemed as we are, we need the application of the love ideal to the more specific contingencies of life. For this reason, the Church, as a teacher of morals, must be cognizant of the radical Gospel demands on the one hand while, on the other, it must be fully aware of the existential situation and needs of its members. A fine example of such an application of the words of Jesus to specific circumstances is to be found in the Sermon on the Mount, which we will now discuss briefly.

THE SERMON ON THE MOUNT
(Mt 5 - 7; cf. also Lk 6:20-49)

Difficult though it may be to formulate the ideals of the Kingdom into a moral code or ethic, the Gospels themselves offer an extended illustration of the meaning of true discipleship in the Sermon on the Mount. This collection of sayings embodies in a special way the "ethical teaching" of Jesus, at least as visualized by Matthew. Within the "good news," we have here a part of the "good advice" of Jesus.

After nineteen centuries the Sermon on the Mount still haunts people. They may praise it or curse it; they may look at it as an impossible ideal or a possible dream. But ignore it, they cannot. Its words are still powerful to rebuke or to inspire. What is the truth about the Sermon on the Mount? And what is its relevance for us as we live in different times, confronted with vastly different problems?

There are actually two great "Sermons" in the Synoptic Gospels: Luke's was "on the Plain," while Matthew's was "on the Mount." Both "Sermons" are collections of the separate sayings of Jesus, spoken at different times and in different contexts, and then arranged differently by Matthew and Luke to accommodate the needs of their respective audiences. Both "Sermons" exemplify the shaping and molding process of the original Jesus material by the early apostolic community, and the subsequent compositional work of the evangelists (Chapters 2 and 3). While both begin with the Beatitudes and end with the parable of the house builder, Luke's account is much shorter. Matthew's longer version incorporates many sayings found scattered throughout Luke's Gospel. While Matthew's "Sermon on the Mount," adapted specifically to Jewish Christians, portrays Jesus as a new Moses giving a "new teaching" (*torah*) to his "new people," Luke's "Sermon on the Plain," adapted to Gentile audiences, portrays Jesus as the vindicator of the poor, the needy and the outcasts of society.

The focus of our attention will be Matthew's version because he deals more directly with attitudes toward the law. His collection of the disparate sayings of Jesus, organized into an organic whole, was probably used as a pre-baptismal catechetical instruction for

Jewish converts. Before baptism, candidates would have to be instructed in the goals and ideals of the "Kingdom way." The central theme is righteousness (sometimes translated "holiness," "good conduct," or even, "virtue," "innocence"). "I tell you, unless your righteousness greatly exceeds that of the scribes and Pharisees, you'll never get into the Kingdom of Heaven" (Mt 5:20). For Matthew, "righteousness" or "holiness" means that conduct which is right and pleasing before God and which fulfills God's will. He then goes on to illustrate the "righteousness" proper to a disciple who has undergone conversion. In a certain sense, the Sermon on the Mount embodies all the qualities and characteristics of the reign of God already discussed in this chapter.

The pivotal point is the style of life or proper way of conduct expected of a disciple, contrasted with the attitudes of the scribes, Pharisees, and others not of the Kingdom. The entire sermon is subdivided into three major areas of contrast:

1. Matthew 5:21-48   the right way of interpreting the Scriptures in contrast with that of the scribes
2. Matthew 6:1-18   the right way of spirituality as contrasted with that of the Pharisees
3. Matthew 6:19-7:27   general principles of right conduct as contrasted with the lifestyle of those who are not of the Kingdom

The entire context is one of discipleship. The Sermon on the Mount is not a detailed ethical code, nor a catalogue of virtues to be cultivated, but simply a series of illustrations about God's demands in some concrete circumstances of life. The Christian is called to be the salt of the earth, the light of the world through signs of reconciliation, purity, concern for others, love of enemies, genuine prayer, faith in God's providence. The emphasis is always on attitudes, outlook, a quality of response characteristic of discipleship. Perhaps some Christians are disappointed in the absence of specific laws. Aren't these words too idealistic? How can they ever be applied to our own life situation?

The question may be more acute. Since the moral demands

of Jesus are so radical and seemingly impossible, can anyone really abide by them? Do we not have an impossible ideal? Is it always possible to turn the other cheek? How far do we go? How do I forgive the murderer, the rapist, the mugger, the spouse or child abuser, the drug pusher on the corner who is destroying the lives of our children? How can a father of a family not worry about his livelihood, about food and clothing for his wife and children? How can anyone tell me to look at the provident way the birds of the air are cared for, when I am faced with exorbitant medical bills and loss of a job? Is there anyone who follows such an ethic?

The Sermon on the Mount is more than rhetoric. Jesus indicates the *goal* and *direction* that should characterize the life and actions of his followers. "Give to everyone who asks" is unreal, but such a demand indicates a permanent quality of concern for those who are less fortunate than ourselves. In certain instances anger may be justified — even psychologically healthy — but the ultimate goal should be reconciliation. A prudent provision for the material welfare of one's family is important, but gross material-ism is hardly compatible with trust in God's providence. Self-defense may be necessary when the innocent are attacked, but ultimately the movement toward peace must prevail. In other words, in spite of its phraseology, so typical of the Semitic way of speaking, the Sermon on the Mount is to be taken very seriously because of the general orientation, outlook and vision it indicates. Perhaps we can highlight some of the more important character-istics of the ethic of Jesus as presented in the Sermon on the Mount.

It Is a Religious Ethic

Faith is the basic premise for living according to the spirit of the Sermon on the Mount. It is an expression of the practice and conduct of those who have accepted the "good news" of God's saving reign revealed by Jesus. Therefore, let all who accept this rule of God live in a new way, the "Kingdom way."

In Catholic tradition of the past, a distinction was made between those who followed the evangelical counsels and those who lived by precepts. The unfortunate implication drawn was that only those who accepted the vows of poverty, chastity and obedience, practically speaking those who belonged to a religious community, lived by the "evangelical" spirit of the Sermon on the Mount, while others lived by precepts. However, living by the precepts of the Gospel is also evangelical.

Furthermore, the distinction between counsel and precept is not securely founded in the Gospels. To the rich young man who asked about the requisites for eternal life (Mk 10:17-22; Mt 19:16-20; Lk 18:18-23), Jesus enjoined the practice of the commandments. When the young man responded: "Teacher, I've obeyed all these from my youth; what else do I need to do?" Jesus answered: "If you want to be perfect, go sell your possessions and give to the poor and you'll have treasure in Heaven. Then come and follow me."

This passage has been justifiably used to provide a Gospel basis for the tradition of the "religious life" which has a long pedigree in Christianity. However, religious life is not a call to a higher form of Christianity, but to a distinct way of life, which should proclaim more of the "pilgrim" character of the Kingdom. The distinction is not between higher or lower spirituality, but between different approaches to the same goal: sharing in the fullness of God's life in Christ. Lay ministry and religious life are simply different avenues of approach to the same destination.

Vatican Council II's *Dogmatic Constitution on the Church* (ch. 5, par. 29-42) emphasizes the universal vocation of *all* Christians to the fullness of Christian life, thereby restoring a healthy respect for the spirituality of lay people, and offsetting any spiritual elitism which has no foundation in the Gospels.

It Is a Disciple's Ethic

The Sermon on the Mount is fundamentally a disciple's ethic; it is directed to those who have said "yes" to the revelation of God's reign. Contrary to the opinion of those who look upon the Sermon as a blueprint for an ideal society or a model for a Utopian type of existence, the Gospel writers view it more as a direction to be taken by people who are prepared to make the venture of discipleship. It moves from what you are ("light of the world," "salt of the earth") to what you should *do*.

But that direction does not necessarily make the moral response of a Christian better or more effective than that of a non-Christian. In other words, is there anything distinctive in this "Kingdom ethic" that is found nowhere else? Is this ethic better than the ethics, let us say, of Jews, Buddhists or, for that matter, secular humanists? The answer to both these questions need not be the same.

The distinctive attribute of the Kingdom ethic — and this applies more broadly to the Christian ethic as well — is the person of Jesus Christ. The Christian's ethical behavior is distinctive because it is based on a vitally new relationship with God in the person of Jesus Christ, and is made explicit at the moment of genuine conversion, even if this is not explicit in each and every moral act. The uniqueness of a Christian's moral response is the explicit Christian consciousness in coming to a moral decision.

But as far as content, the high ideals enunciated in the Sermon on the Mount are also found in non-Christian ethical codes. The Golden Rule of Matthew 7:12: "Whatever you want others to do for you, do so for them as well" is also a Golden Rule in Judaism. In fact, it was appropriated from Judaism! As far as content, the Christian and the non-Christian share basically the same ethical attitudes, values and goals. Non-Christians are as capable of selfless love, a spirit of self-sacrifice, showing concern for those in need, a capacity to turn the other cheek as are Christians. Christian policemen, lawyers, politicians and civil servants do not necessarily demonstrate a more acute moral sensitivity than do their non-Christian counterparts. If Christian ethical behavior is so superior, one is hard put to explain the extermination of six million Jews during World War II in a supposedly Christian nation. Whether the Christian community *ought* to give witness to a keener moral leadership to the entire world, because of the unambiguous demands of Jesus Christ, is quite another question.

It Is a Prophetic Ethic

Christ's thinking as represented in the Sermon on the Mount is closer to that of a prophet than a lawyer. It was a sermon that was preached, not an act that was passed. It does not lay down rules; it opens up principles. It does not enact; it interprets. Certain scribes and legalists suggested that one's character is determined by conduct, and that what must be done is to frame a code of morals telling people how they must act in each and every situation.

Jesus' approach is different. Like the prophets, he is more concerned about persons and principles, not acts. He finds the secret of proper living, not in obedience to a multiplicity of rules and regulations, moral standards imposed from without, but in the spontaneous activity of a transformed character. He enunciates aims and ideals which ought to govern the lives of men and women living in that new order of grace which Jesus calls the Kingdom of God.

It Is an Incomplete Ethic

Many ethical problems of vital consequence to people of our times were never broached in the Sermon on the Mount. Christians may have wished that Jesus had spoken some authoritative words about population control, family planning, euthanasia, capital punishment, environmental issues or so many of the complicated questions arising from the scientific and technological advances of our times. Nothing is mentioned in the Sermon on the Mount about racism, women's liberation, or the obligations of wealthier nations to the people of the Third World. In fact, there is little of what is generally referred to as "social ethics." These were simply not vital issues in first century Palestine.

In light of all that has been said already about the nature of the Sermon on the Mount, one could not expect a complete set of ethics applicable to all of the complex situations arising in future generations. The Gospel writers used the norm of Jesus' life and sayings as a basis for their moral interpretations, but not in a slavishly literal way. They resorted to the "mind of the Lord," when new moral situations developed which were not expressly treated by Jesus during his ministry.

For example, Matthew writing about fifty-five years after the death of Jesus, was already making adjustments based on the mind of the Master for unique situations of marriage within certain close degrees of kinship, which were not dealt with expressly by Jesus (compare Mt 5:32 and Mt 19:3-9 with the earlier version of Mk 10:2-12). Neither was there an explicit commandment of the Lord for Paul's solution to the problem of marriage between a believer and a non-believer who wished to separate (1 Cor 7:12-16). In other words, Paul, like the Church of subsequent ages, had to draw on more than just the words of Jesus.

The "Kingdom ethic," and the entire Christian ethic, for that matter, is a developing ethic. While Christians must always reach back to the radical demands of Jesus, the application is always made in the context of diverse historical and cultural circumstances, those of the first century being vastly different from our own. If the Christian ethic is a developing one, then the Church, the legitimate interpreter of tradition, must continually reexamine its moral formulation by re-presenting anew the demands of Jesus and then apply them to the continually changing circumstances of the modern world.

SOME CONCLUDING THOUGHTS

In times past, traditional Catholic morality may not have given sufficient attention to the radical Gospel demands of Jesus. At times too little was asked and, consequently, too little was given in return. In popular Catholic thinking, ethical demands were reduced to a comparatively few universal norms to be followed by all: the Ten Commandments, the Precepts of the Church, virtues to be practiced, vices to be avoided. The loud and clear demands of a genuine, personal and heart-filled response to the full dimensions of the Gospel were conspicuously absent.

Many norms of the past gave an excessively negative tone to

Christian life, and their performance could easily lull one into a false sense of security. One got the impression that as long as certain laws and obligations were observed, very frequently those pertaining to authority and sex, salvation would be assured. It seemed so clear: follow the rules and you will be saved; violate them, and you will be condemned. Obviously this is an oversimplification. However, certain attitudes of the past concerning the observance of the law would clearly recall a certain pharisaic smugness and complacency condemned by Jesus.

At other times the Church, as the legitimate teacher of morals, may have temporized, soft-pedalled, or deemed it necessary for social or cultural reasons to accommodate temporarily, as in the case of racial equality, the rights of women, or in establishing conditions for a just war. However, when the Gospel demands are the norm, the dynamic thrust must always be toward freedom, the clear affirmation of the personal value and God-given rights of each and every individual, and a radical move toward peace for all.

At times the Church may have absolutized and legislated too much. One has to ask then, just how much is left to personal judgment and conscience? If Gospel morality is our response from the heart, the Church as a teacher should propose rather than impose. She must never hesitate to re-present the radical demands of Christ, but this must be done in such a way that the ideal in question is the ideal of Christ. For this reason, traditional moral questions when exposed to the sharp light of the Gospel demands are being reevaluated. Not all of the past was bad; certainly not all of the new is good. In anxious and confused times like our own, however, there is need more than ever for a reformulation of Christian morality on the basis of the Gospels.

In conclusion, we must never forget that the "Kingdom ethic" is for those who have accepted Jesus as Lord and Savior, for those who have accepted the reality of the Kingdom in their lives, and for those who are, thereby, ensured of the help and power of the Holy Spirit. We are not asked to scale the heights of the Sermon on the Mount by our own unaided powers. But these standards ought to be before us when making personal moral decisions. The law is necessary as a practical guideline to help unaided reason;

it's a human attempt to formulate the radical demands of the Gospels. But the law is not an absolute. Even if none of us reaches the heights to which we are summoned by Christ, the "Kingdom ethic," especially as illustrated in the Sermon on the Mount, indicates the tension between the ideal and the actual, which must ever mark the life of Christ's disciple in this world. Though we, no more than the first disciples, can ever hope to reach this ideal in a fallen world, we are summoned day by day, with the help of the Holy Spirit, to make that effort. To know Christ is to try and respond to his loving demands day by day.

QUESTIONS FOR DISCUSSION

1. Has this chapter contributed in any way to your better understanding of Christian morality? How? What questions does it raise?

2. In what areas, if any, do you find the greatest contrast between current moral tendencies and the traditional moral views of the past? To what do you attribute these changes?

3. How do you regard the Ten Commandments? What kind of a role do they play in your ethical attitudes?

4. What do you consider the foremost qualities of a person who responds in the "Kingdom way"?

5. Do most Christians consider themselves doing God's work in the ordinary human confrontations and commonplace tasks of everyday life?

6. Does traditional Catholic morality place too much emphasis on the "other-worldly" attitude in life? Or is it too concerned with the present?

7. Is it really possible to practice fully the "love commandment" of the Gospels? Or is it unreal?

8. What attitudes or qualities of lifestyle stand out in sharpest

focus from your reading of the Sermon on the Mount
(Mt 5 - 7)?

9. If you are a lay person, do you see your response to God as
different from that of religious? How? If you are a priest or
religious, do you see it different from that of lay people?
How?

10. Is Christian ethical behavior superior to that of non-
Christians? How?

11. How do you understand the role of the Church in the
formulation of your moral decisions?

12. How do the present conditions of our society influence
moral decisions?

Chapter VIII

THE RESURRECTION

Mark 16:1-20; Matthew 28:1-20; Luke 24;
John 20 - 21; 1 Corinthians 15

*C*hristians are called "Easter People" because of their faith in the Risen Lord. In the Christian tradition, even more important than the message of Christmas is the Easter proclamation: God has raised Jesus from the dead! He has exalted him as Lord over all the world and revealed him to his Church as the Living One. The Spirit of the Risen Lord now continues to vitalize his followers. Their lifestyle is, or should be, a joyful commentary based on the conviction that he is risen. Such is the basic claim of "Easter People."

Indeed, so basic is the resurrection to our faith that we can say with St. Paul: "If Christ didn't rise, then everything we proclaimed is in vain, and so is your faith" (1 Cor 15:14). What he means is that Jesus, by his resurrection, has overcome death and has poured forth the power of the Holy Spirit, thus making faith and Christian commitment possible. By sharing in the Spirit of the Risen Lord, the Christian has the means to overcome death, and now lives with the promise of abiding life. Without Easter, there is no Pentecost; and without the coming of the Holy Spirit there is no Church, no Gospel, no Sacraments and no ongoing life of Grace.

In the very first chapter, on oral tradition, we saw how the nucleus of the earliest Christian preaching revolved around the death and resurrection of Jesus. "He who was crucified has been

121

raised." The earliest preaching was, in fact, a challenge to a decision and to a new way of life. The Gospel writers were firmly convinced that Jesus, the long-awaited One, was, indeed, the Messiah. They were saying in so many words: "We believe. Will you take that risk of believing? Will you be willing to undertake a radical renewal of your lives, and be baptized in Christ Jesus?" They asked, not a little, but a great deal.

The Gospels are, in effect, a presentation of the Jesus event intended to provoke a decision of faith. The entire life and ministry of Jesus, his message of the Kingdom proclaimed in parables and dramatized in miracles, his passion and death, his role as Lord and Savior are described in light of the basic conviction that he was raised from the dead, and that he continues to live in his Church. The Gospels are really a portrayal of Jesus as seen through the prism of the Easter faith of the early Christian community. Without the resurrection, there would be no written Gospels. The spirit of Easter pervades the Gospels and makes them a life-giving word, different from any other form of literature. The resurrection of Jesus is the supreme intervention of God in human existence. It is the decisive ground for the proclamation of the "good news," and the basis for our self-identity as followers of Jesus Christ.

DIFFICULTIES ENCOUNTERED

We need not concern ourselves here with the many and sometimes bizarre opinions denying the resurrection of Christ. Some of them are premised on certain philosophical assumptions which simply do not allow for the possibility of life after death. Other well-worn theories of fraud, deception or theft of Jesus' body by the disciples are now *passé*. The same could be said for the hypothesis of massive self-delusion on the part of the disciples, or the comparative religion approach, which sees similarities between the resurrection of Jesus and the myths of dying and rising gods.

Certain modern revivals differ from previous theories only in the remarkable ingenuity and creative imagination of their authors. For example, Hugh Schonfield's *The Passover Plot* has Jesus deliberately contrive to be given a soporific potion to put him into a deathlike trance. After a few hours in the tomb, he regained consciousness and then appeared to his disciples. John Allegro's *The Sacred Mushroom and the Cross* is even more bizarre. According to the author, Jesus never existed, but was a hallucinogenic vision seen by the disciples after ingesting a potion of a small red mushroom, the *Amanita Muscaria*.

Our concern, however, is not fanciful imagination or subjective hypothesis, but the testimony of the Gospel text. What do the Gospels tell us about the Risen Lord? How did the writers project the resurrection into the picture of the historical Jesus? What did the resurrection mean for them? What does it mean for us?

Some Language Problems

Before we examine the Gospel accounts of the resurrection in greater detail, some introductory comments should be made about "resurrection language." What do we mean by the expression "resurrection from the dead"? Since the experience of rising from the dead is an unusual one, to say the least, we must fall back upon metaphors and analogies. "Resurrection from the dead" has a certain metaphorical quality; it uses imagery to convey a reality none of us have yet experienced. From the experienced reality of awakening from sleep, we build an analogy or metaphor of waking from the dead, a non-experienced reality. Just as we rise from sleep in the morning, in a similar way those who are dead shall rise. What better way to describe it? St. Paul, who certainly gave much though to this matter, frequently uses the word "sleep" when speaking of death (cf. 1 Th 4:13, 15; 1 Cor 15:6, 20, 51).

In following the analogy of sleep and rising, one could be tempted to think that the resurrection from the dead is a simple resuscitation of a corpse, a return to life of someone who has died. Many Christians confuse resurrection with some kind of reanimation. But the resurrection of Jesus is unlike the raising to life of the daughter of Jairus or the son of the widow of Nain or Lazarus, because it is more than a simple restoration to life of a body once dead. It is not reanimation, nor is it a reinfusion of life into a corpse not yet decomposed.

The resurrection of Jesus is different. His corpse is not restored to ordinary life. His risen body implies a transformation to a new form of existence beyond the limitation of space and time. The term "resurrection" is a feeble attempt to explain in human words the unique eschatological event by which Jesus Christ was elevated from the tomb to a new form of life. Theologians refer to it as the "glorified state," because it reached beyond the pale of human existence and shares in the glory of God's own life. When speaking of God's life, one can only fall back on metaphors and analogies.

Paul was struggling with the same language problem, as all of us do, when trying to explain the nature of the resurrected body (1 Cor 15:35-36). He speaks of a transformation into a "spiritual body" from a physical one, a transformed existence which we mortals have not yet experienced. Again he falls back on metaphors: "What you sow isn't the body as it will be — it's a bare kernel, perhaps of wheat or something of that sort. God gives it the body He's chosen for it, and each type of seed has its own body" (1 Cor 15:37-38).

Certain modern interpreters have translated the expression "resurrection from the dead" into purely subjective or non-corporeal categories, supposedly to make them more congruent with the thought patterns of today's society. The resurrection of Jesus in such a case merely expresses a spiritual truth, but not an historical reality. He lives. His power, his abiding influence and his cause continue in the lives of his followers. Jesus' resurrection, then, may be likened to the powerful influence on one's life of a recently departed loved one, a wife or a parent, or perhaps some strong religious or political personality. According to the advocates of such a theory, the description of the Risen Lord in terms of corporeal resurrection was the only way the Gospel writers could convey the concept of immortality to a Jewish audience. While such a reduction of the Easter event to a purely spiritual reality requires qualified comment, we must first examine the New Testament evidence.

Testimonies to the Risen Lord

Before it was ever narrated, the resurrection was preached. It was the initial proclamation of the apostolic preachers and missionaries after the Pentecost experience. "You killed this man [Jesus]... yet God raised him and released him from the throes of death" (Ac 2:23-24; 4:10; 5:30-31; 10:39-40). These earlier accounts and those in Paul's letters, focus on the essential proclamation of the death and resurrection of the Lord. The Gospel narratives, written many years afterwards, were already highly embellished and had a tendency to underline the bodily appearances of Jesus, a tendency that became quite pronounced by the time we get to John's Gospel toward the end of the first century A.D.

St. Paul's first letter to the Corinthians, composed some twenty-five years after the actual event, offers the earliest written evidence that we have attesting to Christ's resurrection. His account is somewhat like a creedal formulation or a catechetical summary which he himself did not compose, but which he "handed on" or "handed down" (a technical expression in Judaism for the faithful transmission of tradition) to his readers. If Paul was "handing down" a tradition which he had received, it must have already been circulating throughout Palestine when he visited Jerusalem shortly after his conversion. Scholars have placed this pre-Pauline formula back to within six years after the actual events, perhaps around 36 A.D. Paul writes:

"I handed down to you as of primary importance what I, in turn, had received, namely that Christ died for our sins in accordance with the Scriptures, that he was buried, that he rose again on the third day in accordance with the Scriptures, and that he appeared to...." (1 Cor 15:3-5).

What follows is a list of witnesses, six different groups, beginning with Cephas and ending with Paul himself.

Paul is not so much concerned about proving the truth of Christ's resurrection, which he takes for granted, but rather about convincing the Corinthians that all will rise from the dead as Christ did. In support of his argument, he never mentions the finding of an empty tomb, the witness of the women, the presence of angels, nor, for that matter, does he offer any detailed description of the resurrection. He simply proclaims it. Not concerned with the material or corporeal aspect of the Risen Lord, as were the Gospel writers, he concentrates all of his attention on the spiritual aspects of the event and the significance it has for believers.

In 1 Cor 15:8, Paul presupposes that the appearances he had of the Risen Lord were of the same character as the appearances made to the other apostles. "Last of all he appeared to me as well, to one born at the wrong time, as it were." But his encounter with the Risen Lord takes place on the road to Damascus. Is his "seeing" the same as that of the other apostles? The report of his own encounter with the Risen Lord on the road to Damascus appears in three different versions (Ac 9:1-22; 22:3-21; 26:1-23). Though the three accounts differ in accidentals, substantially they are the same. For Paul, the external form which the self-disclosure of the Risen Lord took included both a visionary and an auditory element, but the inner meaning of the encounter was a communication of the Lord as Risen, and a call to a particular mission. The appearances were not in their innermost essence open to objective verification but revealed the significance of Jesus as Lord, a revelation beyond space and time, one that cannot be adequately captured in "this world" language.

The problem is not made easier when we pass from the writings of Paul to the Gospels. Our discussion will include the so-called "Markan Appendix" (Mk 16:9-20), which is generally regarded as a later addition to the abrupt termination of Mark's Gospel, although the Roman Catholic Church has always accepted it as canonical and inspired. We will also incorporate into our discussion the Gospel of John, to fill out the entire picture of the resurrection of Christ as viewed by the Gospel writers.

THE TESTIMONY OF THE GOSPELS

The reader's first impression on examining the six distinguishable accounts of the resurrection in the four Gospels is one of confusion, because of the many discrepancies in detail (Mk 16:1-8; Mt 28:1-20; Lk 24; Mk 16:9-20; Jn 20 and 21). The accounts do not present a cohesive and homogeneous picture. Attempts at establishing a logical, orderly, step-by-step sequence of events have generally proven to be a frustrating enterprise. The location of the appearances differs; there is no clear-cut chronological or logical ordering of events; the number of women visiting the tomb varies, as do the women themselves.

The accounts of the appearances in Jerusalem say nothing of the appearances in Galilee (Lk 24; Mk 16:9-20; Jn 20), while the Galilean accounts seem to rule out prior Jerusalem appearances to the Eleven (Mt 28:1-20; Jn 21; Mk 16:1-8). An attempt at integrating the various details into one smooth-flowing, logical account is almost impossible. How many women came to visit the tomb? Who were they? How many angels were present? Were they sitting or standing or both? Obviously, we are dealing with popular narratives that have undergone a good deal of embellishment. But, although each of the Gospel writers describes the event in his own inimitable way, they are all basically saying the same thing: Jesus has risen!

How does one explain so many discrepancies? We must recall again that the resurrection event was first proclaimed before it was ever recorded. There was no explanation of the nature of the event, only a declaration: He has risen! It is not possible to provide the same kind of "proof" for the resurrection as for the death of Jesus. While the Passion account practically demands a consecutive, step-by-step progression from the arrest of Jesus in the Garden of Gethsemane to the crucifixion, the same does not hold true for the resurrection. The substance of the various accounts has a double aspect: the appearance of the Risen Lord to the Eleven, and their reception of the mission mandate to continue the proclamation of the Kingdom of God.

Each of the evangelists preserved that memory of an appearance to the apostolic leaders which best suited his purposes. Each writer was a partial witness to a larger picture, selecting only those aspects which best fitted his general mosaic of the Risen Lord. All gave the impression that the appearance was the first, but as far as substance and function were concerned, the six accounts focused on the central appearance to the Eleven and the commission they received from the Risen Lord.

Furthermore, the resurrection or glorification of Christ's body was not an empirically observable event. There were no eye-witnesses to tell us exactly what happened; there were no photographers on the scene. The New Testament claims the resurrection was an act of God, but nowhere does it attempt to describe the event itself. (In practically all instances, the underlying Greek expression emphasizes the role of the Father in raising the Son: "He [Jesus] was raised." Such a translation is not meant to deny the divinity of Christ by any means. It simply underscores God's activity in the resurrection of Jesus.) No one actually saw the resurrection, in spite of the many subsequent artistic and poetic efforts to depict it. The farther away we get from the actual event, the greater attempt there is to flesh it out with detail. The evangelists were doing somewhat the same; they were trying to paint into words an event which did not lend itself to objective and scientific scrutiny.

If the resurrection were the same as the resuscitation of a dead body to life, the matter would be different. But how is it possible to observe by the senses the phenomenon of a living person sharing in the glory of God? The transformed character of the Risen Lord is affirmed, but we can only comprehend and accept it through the gift of faith. The Church has always preferred to call it a "mystery." Even with these difficulties, we must still examine the evangelists' testimony, upon which Christians base their faith in the Risen Lord.

Since the Gospels nowhere claim that anyone saw the actual resurrection, and no attempt is made to describe it, the fact hinges on the validity of two points of evidence:

1. The experiences of those who encountered the Risen Lord.
2. The missing body, or the empty tomb.

THE APPEARANCES OF THE RISEN LORD IN THE GOSPELS

1 Cor 15:3-8 indicates the existence of an earlier tradition about the appearances of the Risen Lord to certain privileged witnesses. Mention is made of Cephas (Peter), the Eleven, 500

brothers at once (most of whom were still alive, although some had already "fallen asleep"). Then, as if to dispel any lingering doubts, Paul adds that he was seen by James, all of the apostles, and then lastly, by himself.

The Gospel accounts dealing with the appearances of the Risen Lord try to flesh out and give further meaning and significance to these earlier traditions. Writing at least ten to twenty years after Paul, if not more, they show a marked tendency to emphasize the bodily appearances of Jesus. In graphic and illustrative fashion, they try to communicate to their audiences the significance of the expression: "He was seen." They are intent on showing that the Jesus who was, is now the Risen Lord. There is a development beyond the simpler, unembellished accounts of the appearances mentioned by Paul. The Gospel writers are groping for adequate space and time terminology to convey a reality that was basically beyond space-time concepts.

They wanted to communicate to their readers that the Risen Lord, who appeared to certain privileged witnesses, was not a ghost, or a figment of the imagination, or a product of mass hallucination, or a subjective vision, but Jesus the Lord who continued to live, but in a new and transformed way. How could one convey the conviction that the Risen Lord now shared in the glory of God? Certainly not by referring to one's own experience, since resurrected life is foreign to the realm of human experience. The disciples were assured of the fact of the resurrection, even if they had not witnessed it personally. That the Risen Lord appeared to chosen disciples was also certain. But they had to wrestle for the right words and symbols to communicate the nature and character of these appearances. For them, even more important than *what* exactly happened was their interpretation of *why* it happened.

With our twenty-first century scientific mentality, we are, of course, curious about the actual resurrection event. How did it happen? What were the details? The Gospel writers, however, were more interested in revealing the *sign*-ificance of the event. They are trying to tell us what the reality of the Risen Lord meant to them and, implicitly, what it should mean for us.

As previously stated, two qualities or aspects of the appearances are highlighted in the Gospels, each indicating a different, though related, truth: the recognition of the Lord and the commissioning of the disciples to continue his mission on earth.

In the former, Jesus is recognized by certain witnesses. They recognize a continuity between the Jesus who lived and the Lord who now appeared. He has been raised! He lives! He remains in our midst! The two disciples journeying to Emmaus recognize Jesus in the word and in the breaking of bread (Lk 24:13-35). In the upper room, Jesus shows them his hands and feet. "Touch me and see, because a spirit doesn't have flesh and bones, as you see *I* do" (Lk 24:39). There is an obvious apologetic intent in Luke to show that the Risen One is not a ghost, or a vision, but someone real. In John 20:17, Mary Magdalene recognizes the Lord only after he calls her by name, "Mary," indicating that his word initiates recognition. Apparently, a faith relationship was necessary before she could recognize the Lord in his new state of existence.

On the other hand, even after recognition, there is a difference in the Lord's form of existence. He was not recognized immediately by Mary Magdalene (Jn 20:14), nor by the disciples on the road to Emmaus (Lk 24:16), nor by Peter and his fishing companions (Jn 21:4). Luke tells us he "vanished from their sight" (Lk 24:31), but then he reappeared elsewhere and greeted them (Lk 24:36). In John 20:19, 26, he appeared to the disciples again, although the doors were locked. Obviously the Gospel writers, especially Luke and John, were wrestling with the problem of trying to communicate the "sameness," yet the "otherness" of the Risen Lord. Before commenting on the nature of the corporeal aspects of the Risen Lord, we should first conclude our discussion with some consideration of the mission mandate evidenced in the appearances.

In addition to recognition, the other prominent feature of the resurrection appearances has to do with the commissioning of the disciples. The mission begun by Jesus of proclaiming the Kingdom must now be continued by his disciples. While the mission mandate is clear, each of the Gospel writers communicates it in a different way. Luke mentions the preaching of penance for the remission of sins, an essential feature of the Kingdom message, and a promise of the Spirit (Lk 24:47-49). Matthew conveys a more developed version of the same basic mandate (Mt 28:18-19), but in the words of the baptismal formula used in his day (probably around 75-85 A.D.). Such Trinitarian terminology would not very likely have come from the lips of the Risen Lord, but from Matthew's version of the commission as it was being applied in the churches of his time.

John's account recalls the giving of the Spirit and the power of forgiving sins (Jn 20:22-23). Interestingly, in the Johannine Appendix (Jn 21:1-14), attributable most likely to later disciples of John, there is already a fusion in one and the same account of a recognition of the Lord by the disciples, and the implicit commission to become fishers of men. Further theological over-laying becomes apparent in the meal setting (Jn 21:12-14) which has eucharistic overtones, thereby connecting the presence of the Lord with the early celebration of the Eucharist.

Even if it appears that the various accounts represent different appearances of the Risen Lord at different times and places, more than likely there is only one basic appearance scene. The commissioning of the disciples has been interpreted with some variation by the evangelists to accommodate their own theological purposes, and the specific needs of their audiences. Such flexible application of the traditions about the Risen Lord is quite understandable, especially since all of the variations are portions of one and the same mandate.

The general commission to proclaim the Kingdom would involve all of the dimensions mentioned by the evangelists: a proclamation of the words and deeds of Jesus, baptism and forgiveness of sins, and testimony of the presence of the Holy Spirit in the community of believers. Thus, the words of the Risen Lord in the various appearances need not be taken as recordings of what he actually said, but as verbalizations of the community's understanding of the meaning and implications of the commission given to Peter and the other disciples. Although they may not have been scrupulous about the exact words of commission pronounced by the Risen Lord, the evangelists were quite faithful to its substance.

THE EMPTY TOMB

The other claim to the reality of the resurrection rests on the Gospel testimony of an empty tomb. If the body of Jesus was not in the tomb, can we simply assume he was raised from the dead? Not necessarily. The body may have been stolen, or removed by the disciples and transferred to another place, as some have suggested. Mary Magdalene, for example, thinks the gardener has taken the corpse and placed it elsewhere (Jn 20:15).

But removal or transferral of the body was hardly likely. How could the disciples have removed the body under the watchful eye of the stationed guards and kept it hidden, especially since they were already under suspicion for being the followers of a Messianic pretender? They would have been under constant surveillance.

And if the body still remained in the tomb, how could they have proclaimed so audaciously the incredible fact of their Master's resurrection, when their opponents could easily have refuted their claims by simply pointing to the presence of the body in the tomb? But even with later Jewish polemics against Christians, there is no indication of any such assertion about the presence of a body in the tomb.

The empty tomb is not, of itself, a proof of Jesus' resurrection. Why then do all of the Gospels mention the discovery of an empty tomb by the women? All four evangelists mention that the stone covering the face of the tomb was rolled back. This fact, of itself, does not offer conclusive evidence for the resurrection of Jesus. However, when coupled with the news of the appearances of the Risen Lord to Peter and the others, the empty tomb becomes an argument of congruence or complementarity. Why was the tomb empty? The answer is given in the reply ascribed to the angels: Jesus had risen as he promised.

Although a harmony of the many discrepant details is almost impossible, the more likely course of events was an appearance of the Risen Lord to Peter and the other disciples in Galilee, while in the meantime, the women discovered the empty tomb in Jerusalem. Originally, the two traditions were independent, and their fusion is attributed to the compositional efforts of the evangelists.

Sometimes the opinion is voiced that it makes little difference whether Christ's tomb was empty or not. Faith in the resurrection would still be the same, so the argument goes, even if the body of Jesus decomposed, or even if, by some unlikely chance, the skeletal remains of Jesus of Nazareth were to be found. A comparison is generally made between loved ones who have recently departed and whose power and influence is still keenly sensed, and the abiding influence of the Risen Lord upon his disciples. The resurrection event, then, is reduced to an ongoing power or dynamism, which would stimulate and encourage his followers to continue his mission on earth.

The problem with this is that such an opinion clashes head on with the incontrovertible evidence of the Gospels. The Gospels are quite clear about the empty tomb, even if that fact is not mentioned in the very earliest accounts. Perhaps it makes little difference to the liberal advocates of such a theory whether the body of Jesus remained in the tomb or not, but if we examine the Gospel texts carefully, we must assume that it would have made a world of difference to Peter and the other witnesses who found the tomb empty.

THE HISTORICITY OF THE RESURRECTION

In the resurrection of Jesus Christ we are confronted with a reality which cannot be expressed in any other way than by that symbolic and metaphorical expression of hope beyond death: the resurrection from the dead. However, this statement must be understood properly. Only the name given this event is symbolic. The verbal expressions are metaphorical, but not the reality itself. While human language may falter and prove inadequate when it comes to expressing so unique an event, by this token, one cannot deny the historical value of the resurrection as an event that actually happened.

A few distinctions are in order. While it is true that critical and scientific criteria will never be able to ascertain the *nature* of this event because the transformed life of the Risen Lord lies outside the limits of space and time, nevertheless he was encountered by men and women who were living in space and time. He showed himself to people who were very much part of the historical experience. In this sense, the resurrection is a historical reality.

However, from another standpoint, the Risen Lord was transformed. He shared the life of God; he was glorified. Such other-worldly characteristics lie beyond the scope of objective and scientific examination and are, therefore, to be regarded as "meta-historical," or beyond the pale of history.

Thus the resurrection is the crossing-point of history and mystery, the natural and the supernatural, "this worldly" and "other worldly." While it is a real fact, as a mystery of faith it is not the kind of fact which can be demonstrated with certainty by methods of historical investigation. The resurrection was launched, as it were, into a transcendent orbit from an earthly platform. In the Risen Lord there is a convergence of history and meta-history. To deny at least this historical foundation leads all too easily to a denial of the resurrection event itself.

Any discussion of the nature of the resurrection must take into account an element of continuity with the past, as well as an element of discontinuity. The ultimate truth lies somewhere in between. On the one hand, Jesus, who died and was buried, was seen and recognized by his disciples as risen. His body was not in the tomb; it was missing. In other words, there is a continuity between Jesus of Galilee, who proclaimed the good news of the Kingdom of God, who ministered and healed, who gathered a group of intimate associates to continue his work, and the Christ who is now proclaimed as risen.

But on the other hand, the Risen Christ was different. His body was transformed. Those who knew him did not recognize him immediately as he stood before them. Mark speaks of an appearance in "another form" (Mk 16:12). The Gospels are not speaking of a resuscitation, a return to life of a body once dead, or a reanimation of a former body. Death involves an immediate process of dissolution and decomposition. But the body that had been placed in the tomb was changed; Jesus did not return to ordinary life. There was a transfiguration. Theologians refer to this state as "glorified," sharing in divine life. But how does one explain this?

St. Paul uses an analogy when he speaks of a "spiritual body" as contrasted with a "physical body" (1 Cor 15:44-49). Again he resorts to a metaphor when trying to depict a reality which mortals have not yet experienced. "One sows a seed and what comes up is a stalk of wheat. A man of dust becomes a man of heaven" (cf. 1 Cor 15:42-49). This is the faltering way in which the human mind can express in human terms that Jesus and the Risen Lord are the same, yet different. The spiritual and imperishable body is quite different from the body that was placed in the tomb. We only know the starting point, but not the final goal of the process. It's a changed body. We can see the consequences of the Risen Lord in the experience of his disciples, but beyond that we cannot go. Small wonder that the Church speaks of the resurrection of Jesus Christ as a mystery!

THE RESURRECTION AND THE CHRISTIAN

What does the Gospel proclamation of the resurrection of Jesus Christ mean to us? Does it have any relevance for *our* lives?

For Jesus, the resurrection was not so much a presence in place and time as it was a relationship. It became multi-dimensional and established a new order of reality between God and humankind. As a result, the human experience of God would never be the same as it was before the coming of Christ.

Whereas Jesus preached the nearness of God's Kingdom, the Easter Church preached the personal experience of the Spirit of Christ. The proclaimer now became the proclaimed. The central teaching of the historical Jesus about the Kingdom of God was now heightened to a proclamation of the realm of the Holy Spirit.

For Jesus the resurrection established a new relationship with God his Father. He received the glory that was always his, as if coming back from a long journey for which he was justly rewarded. He was "glorified," that is, he became fully living and life-giving, with an undeniable facility for radiating the world with his grace, for infusing a new, dynamic life into the community of his followers.

This life-giving power comes in the form of the Holy Spirit, and a new relationship is established with us, his people. In a certain sense Jesus Christ came once and for all. He came and he stayed through the Holy Spirit within the body of his disciples. Because of this, our religious situation is fundamentally altered. By the resurrection, his sonship becomes unique, but also, by his life-giving power, our special relationship with God is established. In him we have become adopted sons and daughters of God. It is precisely through this sharing of his life, his Spirit, that we are related in the Christian communion as brothers and sisters. We become members of the one body of Christ. We can pray and talk to God as with a friend because we share in a very special reality made possible by his resurrection. It is through this Spirit that we can say that Christ dwells in our midst, indeed, that it is "no longer we who live, but Christ who lives within us" (cf. Gal 2:20).

If the Spirit of Christ dwells in our hearts, we become as temples, sacred vessels. A law of respect for one another should exist as never before. For one who lives in the Spirit, the Scriptures speak to the heart as the two disciples on the road to Emmaus experienced. For one who shares in the Spirit, Christ becomes present in the breaking of the bread, the Eucharist. For one who shares in the Spirit, Christ is present in the members of his community. For one who has the Spirit, the struggles, anxieties and sufferings of the present are given meaning and direction. One who shares in the living Spirit of Christ can confront an uncertain future with hope. The Lord has risen! He has overcome death! And so shall we. "Do not be afraid," he assures us, "I'll be with you all the days until the end of the age" (Mt 28:20).

Ultimately, belief in the resurrection of Jesus Christ gives meaning to human existence. What for all of us is still to come has been realized in the Risen Lord. Our Lord and brother has made the grade. Can we who share in his Spirit be far behind? If we really believe and truly live by this Spirit, we can experience the Lord already in the here and now, even if only "through a glass darkly." We can continue on our way joyfully, confident that there is still more to come.

QUESTIONS FOR DISCUSSION

1. What is the significance of the resurrection of Jesus Christ in your personal life?

2. Why couldn't the resurrection of Jesus be understood as a resuscitation to his previous physical life?

3. How do you explain the development in the scriptural accounts of Christ's resurrection from the earlier letters of Paul to the later Gospel narratives?

4. Is there a similarity between our sharing of Christ in the Eucharist and the disciples' recognition of Jesus in word and breaking of bread in the Emmaus account?

5. Would it make any difference, as far as the significance of the resurrection, if the skeletal remains of Jesus were somehow found lying in the tomb?

6. How would you understand the assertion: "The words of the Risen Lord spoken in the appearances do not have to be understood as his actual words, but as the early Church's verbalization of the significance of his words"?

7. What is the most effective way for communicating the reality of the resurrection in our own times?

8. What basic vision or attitude in life do you derive from your belief in the resurrection of Jesus Christ?

9. Why is the Easter message one of hope? How can this attitude be communicated most effectively within the Christian community? The world?

SUGGESTED READINGS

In making the following recommendations, the author has tried to choose those publications which will enhance the understanding and appreciation of Gospel readers. These selections are merely a beginning; they do not presume to be a complete list. Hopefully, interested lay people, religious, clergy and students will find in these selections additional useful information pertinent to each chapter.

Useful for Beginners of the New Testament

The Catholic Study Bible, The New American Bible. Donald Senior, Gen. Ed. (New York: Oxford University Press).

The Gospel According to Matthew, Collegeville Bible Commentary, No. 1. Daniel J. Harrington, S.J. (Collegeville: Liturgical Press, 1983).

The Gospel According to Mark, Collegeville Bible Commentary, No. 2. Philip Van Linden, C.M. (Collegeville: Liturgical Press, 1983).

The Gospel According to Luke, Collegeville Bible Commentary, No. 3. Jerome Kodell, O.S.B. (Collegeville: Liturgical Press, 1983).

The Gospel According to John, Collegeville Bible Commentary, No. 4. Neal M. Flanagan, O.S.M. (Collegeville: Liturgical Press, 1983).

The Acts of the Apostles, Collegeville Bible Commentary, No. 5. William S. Kurz, S.J. (Collegeville: Liturgical Press, 1983).

*The Catholic Bible Study Handbook: A Popular Introduction to
    Studying Scripture.* Jerome Kodell, O.S.B. (Ann Arbor:
    Servant Books, 1985).

Key to the Bible. Vol. 3: The New Testament. Wilfrid J.
    Harrington, O.P. (New York: Alba House, 1975).

CHAPTER I
THE BIRTH OF THE GOSPELS

The Historical Truth of the Gospels. 1964 Instruction of the
    Pontifical Biblical Commission (Glen Rock, NJ: Paulist
    Press, 1965).

"Dogmatic Constitution on Divine Revelation" in *The Documents
    of Vatican II.* Walter M. Abbott, S.J., Gen. Ed. (New
    York: Guild Press, 1966), pp. 107-132.

The New Jerome Biblical Commentary. Raymond E. Brown, S.S.,
    Joseph A. Fitzmeyer, S.J., and Roland E. Murphy,
    O.Carm., Editors. (Englewood Cliffs: Prentice Hall,
    1990).

*   *   *   *   *

Brown, Raymond E., S.S., *The Critical Meaning of the Bible.*
    (New York: Paulist Press, 1981).

Collins, Raymond F., *Introduction to the New Testament.* (Gar-
    den City, NY: Doubleday, 1983).

Harrington, Daniel J., S.J., *Interpreting the New Testament.*
    (Wilmington, DE: Michael Glazier, Inc., 1979).

Perkins, Pheme, *Reading the New Testament.* 2nd edition. (New
    York: Paulist Press, 1988).

Reese, James M., *Experiencing the Good News: The New Testa-
    ment as Communication.* (Wilmington, DE: Michael
    Glazier, Inc., 1984).

CHAPTER II
FROM ORAL TO WRITTEN GOSPEL

Fitzmeyer, Joseph A., S.J., *A Christological Catechism: New Testament Answers*. 2nd Revised and Expanded Edition. (New York/Mahwah: Paulist Press, 1991).

Gutgemans, E., *Candid Questions Concerning Gospel Form Criticism: A Methodological Sketch of the Fundamental Problematics of Form and Redaction Criticism*. (Pittsburgh: Pickwick, 1979).

Hayes, John H., and Holladay, Carl R., *Biblical Exegesis: A Beginner's Handbook*. (Atlanta: John Knox, 1982).

Kaiser, Otto, and Kummell, Werner G., *Exegetical Method: A Student's Handbook*. Revised Edition. (New York: Seabury, 1981).

Kereszty, Roch A., O.Cist., *Jesus Christ: Fundamentals of Christology*. (New York: Alba House, 1991).

Lohfink, Gerhard, *The Bible: Now I Get It*. A Form Criticism Handbook. (Garden City, NY: Doubleday, 1979).

McKnight, Edgar V., *What Is Form Criticism?* (Philadelphia: Fortress Press, 1969).

Meier, John P., "Jesus" in *The New Jerome Biblical Commentary*. (Englewood Cliffs, NJ: Prentice Hall, 1990), No. 78, pp. 1316-1328.

Meier, John P., *A Marginal Jew: Rethinking the Historical Jesus* (Garden City, NY: Doubleday, 1991).

CHAPTER III
THE ROLE OF THE EVANGELISTS

Bornkamm, Gunther, *Jesus of Nazareth*. (New York: Harper & Row, 1975).

Fee, Gordon D., *New Testament Exegesis: A Handbook for Students and Pastors*. (Philadelphia: Westminster, 1983).

Keegan, Terence J., *Interpreting the Bible: A Popular Introduction to Biblical Hermeneutics*. (New York: Paulist Press, 1985).

O'Grady, John F., *The Four Gospels and the Jesus Tradition*. (New York: Paulist Press, 1989).

Perrin, Norman, and Via, Dan O., Jr., ed. *What Is Redaction Criticism?* (Philadelphia: Fortress Press, 1969).

Rohde, J., *Rediscovering the Teaching of the Evangelists*. Trans. by D.M. Barton. (Philadelphia: Westminster, 1969).

Chapter IV
The Kingdom of God

Hiers, Richard H., *The Historical Jesus and the Kingdom of God*. (Gainesville: University of Florida, 1973).

Perrin, Norman, *The Kingdom of God in the Teaching of Jesus*. (Philadelphia: Westminster, 1963).

_____, *Jesus and the Language of the Kingdom: Symbol and Metaphor in New Testament Interpretation*. (Philadelphia: Fortress Press, 1980).

Schnackenburg, Rudolf, *God's Rule and Kingdom* (New York: Herder & Herder, 1963; orig. 1959).

Viviano, Benedict T., O.P., *The Kingdom of God in History*. Good News Studies, No. 27. (Wilmington, DE: Michael Glazier, Inc., 1988).

Chapter V
Parables: Words of the Kingdom

Boucher, Madeleine I., *The Parables*. New Testament Message Series, Vol. 7. (Wilmington, DE: Michael Glazier, Inc., 1981).

Donohue, J.R., "The Parables of Jesus" in *The New Jerome Biblical Commentary*, Aspects of New Testament Thought. (Englewood Cliffs, NJ: Prentice Hall, 1990) 81: 59-88.

Fichtner, Joseph, O.S.C., *Many Things in Parables*. (New York: Alba House, 1988).

Funk, R.W., *Parables and Presence: Forms of the New Testament Tradition*. (Philadelphia: Fortress Press, 1982).

Harrington, Wilfrid J., O.P., *Parables Told by Jesus*. (New York: Alba House, 1974).

Jeremias, Joachim, *The Parables of Jesus*. 2nd Edition. (New York: Scribners, 1972).

Lambrecht, Jan, *Once More Astonished: The Parables of Jesus Christ*. (New York: Crossroad, 1981).

Perkins, Pheme, *Hearing the Parables of Jesus*. (New York: Paulist Press, 1981).

Via, Dan O., *The Parables: Their Literary and Existential Dimension*. (Philadelphia: Fortress Press, 1974).

Wilder, Amos N., *Jesus' Parables and the War of Myths: Essays on Imagination in the Scriptures*. (Philadelphia: Fortress Press, 1982).

CHAPTER VI
MIRACLES: SIGNS OF THE KINGDOM

Brown, Colin, *Miracles and the Critical Mind*. (Grand Rapids: Eerdmans, 1984).

Kee, Howard C., *Miracle in the Early Christian World: A Study in Sociohistorical Method*. (New Haven: Yale University Press, 1983).

Latourelle, Rene, S.J., *The Miracles of Jesus and the Theology of Miracles*. Trans. by M.J. O'Connell. (New York: Paulist Press, 1988).

Mussner, Franz, *The Miracles of Jesus: An Introduction*. (Notre Dame, IN: University of Notre Dame Press, 1968).

Sabourin, Leopold, S.J., *The Divine Miracles Discussed and Defended*. (Rome: Gregorian University Press, 1977).

Senior, Donald, "The Miracles of Jesus" in *The New Jerome Biblical Commentary*, Aspects of New Testament Thought. (Englewood Cliffs, NJ: Prentice Hall, 1990) 81: 91-117.

Theissen, Gerd, *The Miracle Stories of the Early Christian Tradition*. (Philadelphia: Fortress Press, 1983).

CHAPTER VII
THE KINGDOM ETHIC

Curran, Charles E., and McCormick, Richard A., eds., *Readings in Moral Theology*. Vol. 4: The Use of Scripture in Moral Theology. (New York: Paulist Press, 1984).

Daly, Robert J., et al., *Christian Biblical Ethics: From Biblical Revelation to Contemporary Christian Praxis*, Method and Content. (New York: Paulist Press, 1984).

Fuller, Reginald H., ed. *Essays on the Love Commandment*. (Philadelphia: Fortress Press, 1978).

Mott, Stephen C., *Biblical Ethics and Social Change*. (New York: Oxford University Press, 1982).

Perkins, Pheme, *Love Commands in the New Testament*. (Ramsey, NJ: Paulist Press, 1982).

Sanders, J.T., *Ethics in the New Testament*. (Philadelphia: Fortress Press, 1975).

Spohn, William C., *What Are They Saying About Scripture and Ethics?* (Ramsey, NJ: Paulist Press, 1984).

Chapter VIII
The Resurrection

Brown, Raymond E., *The Virginal Conception and the Bodily Resurrection of Jesus.* (Paramus, NJ: Paulist Press, 1973).

de la Potterie, Ignace, S.J., *The Hour of Jesus: The Passion and Resurrection of Jesus According to John.* (New York: Alba House, 1990).

Fuller, Reginald, *The Formation of the Resurrection Narratives.* (New York: Macmillan, 1971).

Leon-Dufour, Xavier, *Resurrection and the Message of Easter.* (New York: Holt, Rinehart & Winston, 1975).

Marxen, W., *The Resurrection of Jesus of Nazareth.* (Philadelphia: Fortress Press, 1968).

O'Collins, Gerald. *The Resurrection of Jesus Christ.* (Valley Forge: Judson Press, 1973).

_____, *What Are They Saying About the Resurrection?* (Ramsey, NJ: Paulist Press, 1978).

Perkins, Pheme, *Resurrection: New Testament Witness and Contemporary Reflection.* (Garden City, NY: Doubleday, 1984).

GLOSSARY

Apocalyptic — a literary type featuring a great deal of esoteric, symbolic imagery and characterized by a fascination with the end of time breaking into the near future.

Apologetic Manuals — those theological works whose rational and historical approach tries to "defend" the Christian faith or demonstrate the grounds of its credibility through philosophical and historical arguments.

Biblical Commission — a permanent body of distinguished biblical scholars founded in 1902 by Pope Leo XIII for the purpose of promoting the Catholic study of Scripture.

Cephas — an Aramaic common name which means "rock." It is translated into Greek by the word "petros," whence the English "Peter."

Criticism (Critical Approach) — derived from a Greek verb which means "to judge," this method of interpretation recognizes the Scriptures as historically conditioned and recorded in specific literary forms.

Day of the Lord — the time of the decisive and definitive intervention of God in favor of his people. In the New Testament, it refers to that time when Jesus Christ will bring the present age to its close and make the definite passage into a new future epoch.

Demythologization — interpreting mythical concepts of the Bible into a language having contemporary existential meaning.

Diaspora — a Greek word meaning "dispersion," and used to designate Jewish communities who settled outside Palestine.

Eschatology (Eschatological) — from the Greek word for "end" (*eschaton*). It refers to the belief that a divine act terminates history and inaugurates a new age, a new dimension of reality.

Evangelist — author of a Gospel, even in the broadest sense of authorship; the one who selects from the various traditions about Jesus, arranges them and then gives them final theological interpretation.

Existentialism (Existential) — the view that a person has no essence or nature imposed on him or her but is constituted solely by free and responsible choices. The subjective experience of a person in a given situation becomes the ultimate criterion for decision.

Fundamentalism — an approach to the Scriptures maintained by those who accept a strict, literal, historical account of the biblical record.

Glorified State — in the New Testament, "glory" expresses the divine mode of being. It is generally used to describe the state of the Risen Lord after Easter when he fully shares the life-giving power of his Father.

"Hedge" of the Law ("Fence") — legal opinions and interpretations which advanced the obligations of the Mosaic law well beyond the sense of the words, thus protecting its perfect observance. Such practice became the identifying badge of Judaism.

Hellenistic-Gentile — milieu dominated by Grecian culture and ideals, in contrast to one which is Palestinian-Jewish.

Historical Criticism — a method of interpretation which tries to determine the biblical authors' intended message for the original readers within the context of their historical experience.

Historical Truth of the Gospels — an important instruction from the Biblical Commission issued on April 21, 1964, which recognizes the validity and implications of a three-stage development in the formation of the Gospels.

Historicity of the Gospels — an understanding of the words and works of Jesus as genuinely, reliably and authentically founded upon historical facts.

Infancy Narratives — (Mt 1 - 2; Lk 1 - 2) accounts of the infancy and childhood of Jesus written in a special literary style. They expand the basic data contained in the memory of Jesus' early life by the use of Old Testament allusions and a more developed belief in his divine character.

Inspiration — the collaboration between the divine and the human in the composition of the books of Sacred Scripture. God chose people and, while He employed them, they made use of their own powers and abilities so that, with God acting in them and through them, they committed to writing all those things God wanted. Also, writings "animated" by the Spirit of God.

Johannine Appendix — John 21: an epilogue to John's Gospel written most likely by one of John's disciples and added to the Gospel before it was finally published.

Kerygma — the earliest apostolic preaching about the significance of the death and resurrection of Jesus.

Literary Criticism — that method which studies the New Testament as literature, especially as comprised of literary genres (types) and features found in other literature.

Messiah — the Hebrew term meaning "anointed one." It refers to the long-awaited king and deliverer of the Jews. The word is rendered in Greek by "Christus," whence the English "Christ."

Messianic Psalms — those which deal explicitly or implicitly with the theme of a future deliverer or with features of his person or reign.

Meta-Historical — that which lies "beyond" history and therefore observable, not by scientific inquiry, but solely by faith.

Metanoia — a Greek term meaning "repentance." It refers to the radical change of mind and heart, indeed, to the personal revolution demanded of one who has accepted the Kingdom of God.

Passover — one of the principal Jewish feasts which annually memorializes in ritual fashion God's saving power in freeing the Israelites from Egyptian bondage.

Pentateuch — taken from the Greek meaning "book of five volumes," this term refers to the first five books of the Old Testament.

Reanimation — a restoration to life of a body once dead; revivification.

Righteousness — in the Gospel of Matthew it denotes conduct which is right and pleasing before God and which fulfills his will. In Paul's letters, it denotes God's saving concern for all.

Son of Man — one of the titles used by the early Christians in referring to Jesus and the one used most often by Jesus himself in the New Testament when he wanted to designate himself. It has its roots in the Old Testament (Dn 7) and it is used in the apocalyptic literature of I Enoch and IV Ezra.

Suffering Servant — a title applied to Jesus which interprets his life's work and death as fulfilling the mission of the Servant of Yahweh announced in Isaiah 53.

Synoptic Gospels — the first three Gospels of the New Testament so called because, when placed side by side (synoptic is from the Greek verb meaning "to view together"), they contain a large amount of parallel material. John's Gospel differs in content and structure from these three.

Yahweh — A proper name in Hebrew by which God revealed himself to Israel through Moses (Ex 3:14; 6:3): "I am who am." Out of reverence for this name, the term *Adonai*, Lord, was later used as a substitute. The word "Jehovah" arose from a false reading of Yahweh in the Hebrew text.